Ice Story

Ice Story

Shackleton's Lost Expedition

Elizabeth Cody Kimmel

CLARION BOOKS

NEW YORK

For my husband, Donald

ACKNOWLEDGMENTS

Grateful acknowledgment is made to Philippa Hogg and the Scott Polar Research Institute for their kind assistance.

Thanks also to Sheldon Fogelman, Marcia Wernick, Amanda Junquera, John Clarke, Donald Kimmel, George Kimmel, and Jennifer Greene for their invaluable assistance with this book.

Lastly, special acknowledgment and thanks to Dorothy Briley, who is sadly missed.

CLARION BOOKS

A Houghton Mifflin Company imprint

215 Park Avenue South, New York, NY 10003

Photographs by Frank Hurley and all maps reproduced with the kind permission of the Scott Polar Research Institute.

Photographs on pages 5 and 51 reproduced by kind permisson of Corbis-Bettman.

Designed by Lisa Diercks.

Text type is Fournier with Gill Sans display.

Library of Congress Cataloging-in-Publication Data

Kimmel, Elizabeth Cody.

    Ice Story: Shackleton's Lost Expedition / by Elizabeth Cody Kimmel.

       p. cm.

    Summary: Describes the events of the 1914 Shackleton Antarctic expedition, when the ship the Endurance was crushed in a frozen sea and the men made the perilous journey across ice and stormy seas to reach inhabited land.

    ISBN 0-395-91524-4

    1. Shackleton, Ernest Henry, Sir, 1874–1922—Juvenile literature. 2. Endurance (Ship)—Juvenile literature. 3. Imperial Trans-Antarctic Expedition, 1914–1917—Juvenile literature. [1. Shackleton, Ernest Henry, Sir, 1874–1922. 2. Endurance (Ship) 3. Imperial Trans-Antarctic Expedition, 1914–1917.] I. Title.

    G850 1914 S53K56   1999

    910'.91673—dc21   98-29956

    CIP   AC

Printed in the USA.

CRW 10 9 8 7 6 5 4 3 2 1

Frontispiece: Sir Ernest Shackleton.

We are the fools who could not rest
In the dull earth we left behind,
But burned with passion for the South
And drank strange frenzy from its wind.
The world where wise men live at ease
Fades from our unregretful eyes,
And blind across uncharted seas
We stagger on our enterprise.

—ST. JOHN LUCAS

Contents

Elephant Island.

PROLOGUE

IT WAS EARLY IN THE AFTERNOON ON APRIL 24, 1916. On a barren, rocky beach nestled between a glacier and the pitching, foaming sea stood twenty-two men, their tattered clothing providing little protection against the bitter cold. In the ocean before them, a small wooden lifeboat headed out to sea, its outline dwarfed by the enormous waves crashing down around it. The six men in the boat, under the command of Sir Ernest Shackleton, waved at their comrades who stood on the shore waving back, until the boat disappeared from view. Each feared they might never lay eyes upon the other again.

It is hard to say which group of men faced more danger. Elephant Island was a rocky, forlorn tumble of ice and mountains off the coast of Antarctica. Except for the twenty-two men now standing on its tiny beach, it was completely uninhabited. Not a soul in the world had good reason to suspect these men needed help. Their position was far too remote for them to hope a passing ship might spot them and give rescue. The unrelenting Antarctic winter would soon be upon them, and the desolate coast, a lonely stretch of ice and rock, provided no shelter at all.

In the twenty-two-foot wooden lifeboat called the *James Caird*, Sir Ernest was leading his small crew of men out to the open ocean. More than eight hundred miles away lay South Georgia, an island that was home to a whaling station and a small community of men. There, Shackleton hoped to find help and to organize a rescue party to pluck his remaining men from Elephant Island before the full force of the winter was upon them. Between Shackleton's position and South Georgia lay some of the most savage seas in the world. Ships ten times the size of the *Caird* had been swallowed up without a trace in these waters. Towering waves, as high as ninety feet, crashed unceasingly, and gales raged more often than not. It would take a miracle for Shackleton to reach South Georgia, but as he knew all too well by this time, a miracle was their only hope for survival.

How did these men come to find themselves in such a desperate situation, alone in the treacherous Antarctic wastelands, all their hopes pinned on the seaworthiness of one lifeboat and the courage and ability of their leader?

It was a strange and improbable chain of events that had carried the men this far. The story begins with a great three-masted ship named *Endurance* and a rugged Irishman named Shackleton, whose exploits to the South Pole were already legend. What follows, however, is the story of an expedition made famous because it never happened—a voyage gone so horribly wrong it may be the greatest misadventure the world has ever known.

CHAPTER ONE

A Taste for Adventure

FOR THOUSANDS OF YEARS, THE GREATEST MINDS OF civilization had suspected, theorized, and dreamed of a vast southern continent lying beyond the last outposts of humanity. Long before the theory that the world was round had been proven, this phantom continent appeared on maps as Terra Australis Incognita, the unknown southern land. Antarctica was not sighted by a human being until 1820, when the world at last received concrete proof that Terra Australis existed. But no one knew what lay beyond its coastline of snow and glacier, and by the year 1900, only a handful of men had set foot on the continent's icy shores.

Antarctica took hold of the imagination of the adventurous and would not let go until they sought the place out themselves, or died trying. Naval officers, geologists, artists, doctors, and sailors—men from all walks of life—came together on the first great expeditions to the southern continent. The world waited fearfully and excitedly for news of their return and for stories of what they encountered. In their time, these expeditions of science and exploratory conquest created as much excitement and suspense as did the first trips to outer space in the 1960s. Unlike their astronaut counterparts, however, the polar explorers could spend years on a single expedition, completely out of touch with civilization. While they were gone, their families and the public could only dream of what had become of them.

Ernest Shackleton was a restless, energetic boy who dreamed of doing great and unusual things. He was the elder of two sons in a family with ten children. His parents may have suspected that Ernest was fated to be an explorer when they found him trying to dig his way to Australia by tunneling through their back yard. In a house almost overflowing with children, Ernest's mother and father worked to create a loving and supportive family atmosphere. It was a home offering ample laughter and affection, and even as a very young child, Ernest was completely supported and encouraged by his parents to do whatever he most desired in life. His sisters quite adored their headstrong brother, and they were certainly his first and most zealous fans.

Born in Ireland in 1874, Ernest moved to England with his family ten years later. Much of his early education was provided at home by a private governess. As a boy of ten, Shackleton attended Fir Lodge Preparatory School as a day boy, and three years later he enrolled as a student at Dulwich. By all reports, Ernest seemed bored with school, though he read books and magazines with a passion. It was these first explorations through books that sparked in the little Irish boy a fascination with adventure. At the age of sixteen, Ernest left his home in England for the first of many journeys at sea, where he earned a small wage in the mercantile marine. Facing the complicated rigging of his first ship, a large sailing vessel called *Hoghton Tower*, young Ernest literally set himself to "learning the ropes." The demanding requirements of living and working on such a ship, and the payoff of experience and adventure, agreed with Ernest. After his first voyage working on the *Hoghton Tower*, he signed papers confirming his official commitment to spend the next four years working at sea in the mercantile marine. By

1898, aged twenty-four, he had passed an examination for master, which gave him the qualifications and authority to command a ship of his own should the opportunity arise. He saw much of the world from the deck of a ship, and it was only a matter of time before the call of the greatest and most mysterious continent of the world reached his ears. Antarctica was truly the last great frontier; only recently discovered, and almost entirely unexplored, the continent presented the ultimate challenge to the brave of heart.

It was in this atmosphere of the unknown that Shackleton was waiting when he first heard of an expedition being organized to the South Pole. The leader was to be a young naval officer named Robert Falcon Scott. With the determination he would become known for, Shackleton secured himself a position on the expedition and took his place on board the ship *Discovery*, bound for the southern continent.

Beneath its ice and snow, Antarctica has land and mountains. The mountain in the distance, Mt. Erebus, is actually a volcano. On Shackleton's second expedition to Antarctica in 1907, he and his men were the first reach its summit.

No previous expedition had even come close to reaching the South Pole, a tiny spot on the globe that marks the bottom of the world. Due in large part to his physical strength and great enthusiasm, Shackleton was chosen along with one other man, Dr. Edward Wilson, to join Scott in an overland journey from *Discovery* to the South Pole. While their colleagues waited onboard, the three men departed on foot for the Pole, a team of dogs dragging sledges loaded with food and supplies behind them. Three months later they returned. Every last dog had perished or been killed for food. Scott was dangerously weakened. Shackleton, who only days before had not been expected to live, was seriously ill and broken down. The three men had not reached the Pole. Because of illness, lack of food, and severe weather conditions, they had been forced to turn back while still more than four hundred miles from their goal.

From that first trip Shackleton took home with him some serious lessons about the dangers of polar exploration. Like so many others, however, he was consumed with the need to face the challenge again. Scott, too, would return to Antarctica. In a 1911–12 venture, Scott made a second attempt to reach the Pole and succeeded, only to find the Norwegian flag flying there. The Norwegian explorer Roald Amundsen and his party had beaten Scott by mere weeks, securing Amundsen's place in history as the first man to the South Pole and dashing Scott's hopes of acquiring that same title. This time, Scott was to pay the heaviest price for his efforts. On their return from the Pole, Scott and his men, disappointed, exhausted, and on the point of starvation, took shelter in their tents from a blizzard. Overcome by the cold and lack of food, they lay helpless in their sleeping bags as their strength ebbed. Not one of them survived. When search parties finally reached the expedition tent, they found Scott's journal among his personal belongings. Of Antarctica, the explorer had written, "Great God! this is an awful place. . . ."

It was to this awful place that Shackleton returned to seek his own fate—a place in the history books, death, or both.

CHAPTER TWO

Under Way at Last

As Shackleton prepared for his Imperial Trans-Antarctic Expedition of 1914, he had the luxury of being known as one of the United Kingdom's greatest polar explorers. In 1907 he had led a group to within ninety-seven miles of the Pole, which was a new world record. On the same expedition, his men became the first to climb Mount Erebus, a thirteen-thousand-foot volcano off the Antarctic coast. For these accomplishments he was knighted by the king of England, earning the title *Sir* and securing himself great fame. The Imperial Trans-Antarctic Expedition was to be his third to the southern continent and the second that he was to command.

Since Amundsen had already won the honor of being the first to reach the South Pole, Shackleton felt the one great feat yet unaccomplished was to cross the entire Antarctic continent, some eighteen hundred miles over largely unexplored land. He planned to do this on foot, with teams of dogs to pull sledges of supplies. His team would set out from the shore of the Weddell Sea and head toward the opposite coast, traveling straight through the South Pole and making history in the process. Directly across the continent, another team of men would lay in supplies for the trans-Antarctic team; their ship in the Ross Sea would provide support and a safe haven for Shackleton's arrival. On paper and in person, Shackleton made it seem almost simple, but he knew from experience it would be anything but that.

The unfriendly terrain that makes up Antarctica is almost entirely covered by ice and snow. There is no native human population, and only a small variety of hearty plants and of animals, mostly seals and penguins, can survive there. The lowest temperature ever recorded in history occurred on the continent—a brisk 129 degrees Fahrenheit below zero. Blizzards, characterized by fierce winds and falling or blowing snow, are a frequent occurrence and may last for days.

The exceedingly harsh conditions of the area were known, but this did not discourage the thousands of men who eagerly applied to join Shackleton on his expedition. Of these thousands, Shackleton chose twenty-six, including the man who would act as ship's captain, Frank Worsley. Captain Worsley would later claim that a strange dream of a London street filled with icebergs led him to Shackleton's office, where he promptly requested and was granted his place on the team. The twenty-seventh man was not to appear until the *Endurance* was well out at sea—he had hidden on the ship and joined the party as a stowaway.

Shackleton named his ship *Endurance* partly to honor his family, whose motto was "By endurance we conquer." The *Endurance* was a wooden, three-masted sailing vessel known as a barkentine, measuring 144 feet long and 25 feet wide. The ship had a steam engine and had been specially built by a Norwegian shipyard to withstand the polar ice.

As the ship underwent final preparation for the journey, world events almost forced the cancellation of the expedition. In Austria-Hungary, the Austrian archduke Francis Ferdinand was murdered by a Serb gunman. In the frenzied chain of events that followed across Europe, the tangle of national alliances and rivalries worsened. Austria-Hungary declared war on Serbia. Serbia's ally, Russia, in turn threatened Austria-

On deck of the *Endurance*.
Sled dogs were housed in
kennels on either side of
the deck.

Quarters were cramped below deck, particularly when the men gathered for meals.

Hungary's borders. Throughout Europe, countries divided and chose sides in the conflict, and soon Germany had declared war on Russia and France. The entire structure of Europe seemed on the brink of collapse. On August 5, responding to the threat from Germany, Britain entered what would become known as the First World War. It was an agonizing decision for Shackleton, but he immediately contacted the British Admiralty and offered to put his ship and men at the Admiralty's complete disposal. He received a cable in response from Winston Churchill, saying simply, "Proceed." With that blessing from the First Lord of the Admiralty, the *Endurance* set sail as England prepared for battle.

The *Endurance* made one last stop in the civilized world, at the island of South Georgia, before continuing south in December. By January, as they were approaching the Antarctic Circle, they encountered their first pack ice. Each winter, a vast portion of the ocean surrounding Antarctica freezes, forming pack ice. This ice never completely melts, even in the summer, and settles like an iron blanket around the continent. Large flat pieces of the pack ice break off and form ice floes, which move with massive force and can easily crush a ship. The sea is also crowded with icebergs—enormous chunks of ice that have broken off glaciers or ice shelves and plunged into the sea. These ice monsters, some large enough to be visible from space, can measure over twenty-five miles long and rise more than one hundred feet out of the ocean. If crossing Antarctica was a dangerous exploit, reaching the continent could be just as deadly.

Shackleton had not expected to find ice so far from the continent. He found that the ice was heavier and more plentiful than on his previous expeditions. If he became concerned this early in the expedition, however, he did not share his concerns with his crew. Even those aboard the *Endurance* who had never seen the frozen ocean knew the dangers these conditions posed. A collision with a barrier of ice could rip a hole in their ship and sink them almost instantly. Only two years had passed since an iceberg had sunk the great and supposedly unsinkable ocean liner *Titanic*. The men remembered the tragedy only too keenly. *Endurance* sailed slowly through the ice with all possible caution.

Shackleton and Captain Worsley kept these dangers firmly in their minds as the *Endurance* crept carefully closer to her destination, picking her way through the soup of bergs and floes. When they found an area where the ice was passable, they worked on making a lane through it. This method allowed them to make some progress, until one day in mid-January. Finding their way blocked by a large ice floe, Shackleton decided to wait for a change of wind. Changing wind conditions often served to redirect the movement of the ice floes. No change came, however, for almost a week. During that time, the heavier pack ice had slowly surrounded the ship. Using the combined power of the sails and steam engine, the *Endurance* strained to break free. It was useless. Just a month and a half into their expedition, the *Endurance* and her crew were prisoners, stuck fast in the Antarctic ice.

The *Endurance* struggles against the ice under full sail.

CHAPTER THREE

A Long Dark Winter

I T WAS NOT UNHEARD OF FOR A SHIP TO BECOME FROZEN into the polar ice. During previous expeditions to both the North and South Poles, ships had become stuck, or beset, for months on end. This usually occurred during the polar winter months, and the ship's crew would settle in to wait for the spring thaw. The danger did exist that the ice would press inward against the ship, disabling or even sinking it, but Shackleton had no particular reason to believe that this would happen to the *Endurance.*

One final effort was made in February to break free, the steam engine struggling as the men hacked away at the ice, but it was no good. The ice refroze as fast as they could break it apart. At this point, it was generally accepted that the *Endurance* was stuck for the duration of the Antarctic winter, which occurs during the months of June, July, and August, when most of the world is experiencing summer. The men good-naturedly set about converting the ship for the winter. Some of the crew's quarters were moved to a warmer section of the ship. The dogs, previously housed in kennels on deck, were transferred to new homes on the ice, where the men built "dogloos" of snow blocks to

The dogs in their new quarters.

insulate the kennels. These husky creatures were well insulated with fat and fur and were quite comfortable in their new quarters.

As the temperature dropped, the ice surrounding the ship became increasingly solid, and it was now relatively safe to climb off the ship and travel short distances over the surface. Games of ice soccer were organized, and Shackleton encouraged the exercise, for the coming of winter would soon mean total darkness. In the South Polar Circle, the height of Antarctic summer in January brings twenty-four hours of

Games of ice soccer provided relief from boredom and helped keep the men in shape.

continuous sunlight. The days then grow shorter until the arrival of winter in June, when a month of twilight gives way to the complete darkness of midwinter, and the sun never rises above the horizon. This lack of sunlight had been known to affect explorers severely. In extreme situations, men had been known to lose their minds after weeks in the darkness.

The crew, confident that the ship could break free in the spring thaw, found that their main enemy was boredom. Shackleton's first concern was always the well-being of his men, and he took care to organize a

The crew in costume celebrate Midwinter Day. The comic performances included a lengthy tongue-in-cheek speech by Shackleton praising his own accomplishments. A great feast followed the theatricals.

schedule of entertainment to keep the men in good spirits. Plays and lectures were put together, games were played, and contests took place to determine the ship's worst singer. While the last hours of daylight still lingered, hunting parties were sent out to kill seals, before their numbers moved north to follow the sun. Armed with guns and knives, the hunting parties were greatly successful, and a large supply of fresh meat was laid in for the winter.

By June there was only a brief period of faint light each day at noon. Advantage was taken of these final dim twilight moments to stage a dog derby. Teams of dogs were raced across the ice, the observers laying bets using their precious rations of tobacco and chocolate. Temperatures now routinely fell far below zero, but the exercise on the ice and the heat from the ship's stoves combined to keep the men comfortably warm at most times.

A ferocious blizzard in mid-July packed the ice even tighter around the *Endurance*. They were caught fast, one crewman had joked, like an almond in a chocolate bar. Though beset, the *Endurance* was moving nonetheless. The pack ice as a whole was slowly drifting, thanks to the wind and ocean currents. The *Endurance*, moving with the ice, had traveled more than 160 miles. Below her decks, as the weeks drifted past, Shackleton and his crew waited patiently into September, when they hoped the returning sun would melt the bars of their prison.

CHAPTER FOUR

The Ice Tightens

Before the month was out, it became obvious that something was seriously wrong. Instead of loosening, the ice had actually tightened around them. The currents and prevailing winds were pushing the pack ice—and the *Endurance* within it—toward the Antarctic coast. The land created an impassable barrier and left the pack ice with nowhere to go. As a result, the ice floes forming the pack were forced closer and closer together, and the pressure around the ship slowly increased. Strange noises came from the depths of the ship, as the wood of the decks began to bend upward under the stress.

It was difficult to maintain a routine onboard. The men were now in constant danger and had to be on careful guard. The leisurely nights of singing and buffoonery around the ship's stove were over. The men now watched the progress of the ice anxiously. They could actually feel thuds beneath their feet as the floes pressed closer and closer against the sides of the *Endurance*. The force created by the ice against the ship's hull was equal to countless tons of weight. She was a strong and sturdy ship, built to withstand the severe conditions of the polar seas, but no ship existed that could survive such a powerful onslaught for long.

The ice seemed determined to battle them to the end. Wind and pressure shoved and cracked the pack, piling ice floes one on top of the other, their bulk squeezing the very life out of the *Endurance*. But by October, the vessel remained stubbornly in one piece. Spring had arrived, and Shackleton optimistically gave orders to reorganize the ship for sailing.

Sir Ernest was not naive, and no doubt he was only too aware that his ship stood little chance of remaining seaworthy after the relentless attack of the ice. But Shackleton was a man who was keenly aware of the value of hope and the crucial importance of maintaining good morale and high spirits among his men. Inwardly, he suffered from a deep fear of losing control of his crew. The men had been living virtually on top of one another for months. The ship was beginning to collapse beneath their feet. Shackleton knew he had no hope of leading his men to safety if they became depressed or angry with one another, or if they lost faith in their leader.

He must have been desperately disappointed. His Imperial Trans-Antarctic Expedition had been years in the making. Sir Ernest had devoted every last ounce of his energy to organizing the expedition, traveling around the country raising funds, overseeing every detail, no matter how small. The expedition was to be the crowning achievement of his exploring career. Now the expedition might very well never take place. It was a cruel turn of events, but Shackleton never let his men see his despair. He remained cheerful and commanding, focusing all of his considerable energy on keeping his men alive.

Frank Hurley, the ship's photographer, took this dramatic photograph of the *Endurance* in the midst of the Antarctic night in full moonlight. Presumably some of the light is artificial.

The pressure of the ice caused the *Endurance* to heel to one side. She later righted herself.

While still maintaining that the *Endurance* might be freed from the ice, Shackleton carefully prepared for another outcome: that their ship was going to sink. Whatever happened, he would not be caught unprepared. The men grimly carried out his orders, transferring the most important supplies to the top deck, so that they might be moved onto the ice at a moment's notice.

It was now October 24, and they were ready. Each man knew what

Shackleton, at right,
on deck of the
heeling ship.

Many different types of ice surrounded the *Endurance*. The men called the cotton-like ice formations in the foreground frost-flowers.

was expected of him, and each was prepared when the ice ripped a hole in the ship's stern and the frigid water of the Weddell Sea began to pour into their home.

They fought with every last particle of strength. They pumped and bailed out the water around the clock, using every available man, but the water rushed in faster than they could remove it. Once inside the *Endurance,* the water froze and burdened the ship with weight it was not designed to hold. Over the men's heads, massive wooden beams snapped like matchsticks, making explosive sounds like gunfire. The *Endurance* and her crew fought it out to the last. On the third day, as their strength began to give way, Shackleton gave the order to abandon ship, and his exhausted crew climbed off the *Endurance*. It was a dazed and numb band of men who stood on the ice, watching as their home and only link with the outside world folded like a paper fan before their eyes.

CHAPTER FIVE

A Plan for Escape

In his diary, Shackleton called the Weddell Sea "the worst sea in the world," but he did not express this to his men. He acted with utter confidence, almost defying the fact that they were now stranded on an ice floe off the coast of Antarctica, perhaps a thousand miles from civilization. As he supervised the pitching of the tents and the organization of supplies, he did not remind the men that they were unlikely to be rescued, that they had no radio capable of reaching the outside world, and that no one expected to hear from them for many months. But as always, Shackleton had a plan, and the men gathered around him eagerly to hear it.

They were not the first crew of explorers to encounter trouble in Antarctica, and years ago Shackleton himself had been hired to lay in a supply of food, fuel, and clothing for future castaways. The stores had been deposited on Paulet Island, which Captain Worsley estimated lay some 350 miles from their position. These supplies could provide them with crucial protection from the elements, and there they might await a rescue effort or take further action as Shackleton directed.

Sir Ernest explained that they would travel on foot over the ice for as long as possible, dragging the lifeboats and sledges behind them with

The crew salvaged what
materials they could from
the crushed ship before
setting off across the ice.

the help of the dogs. They would proceed in this way until they found an area of open water. Then they would pack the supplies into the lifeboats and row or sail the remaining distance to Paulet Island.

After months of inactivity followed by the frenzied struggle to save the ship, the men felt greatly relieved to have a plan of action on which to concentrate. Each man was to be responsible for hauling certain items, and the dog teams were readied to pull their loads. Over the next few days, Shackleton made the unhappy decision to shoot the youngest and weakest dogs, who lacked the strength and training to be of any assistance. The ship's cat, Mrs. Chippy, was also killed. It was a difficult decision, but Shackleton knew that unless an animal was capable of helping them carry their supplies, they could not afford to share their valuable and limited stores of food with it. The dogs were killed quickly, and well out of view of their companion animals. Within several months, the last of them would be killed. Many of the crew had grown deeply fond of the dogs, and losing their companionship was to be one of the most difficult hardships the men would endure.

That night they settled into their sleeping bags, between four and eight men to a tent, and tried to get enough sleep to prepare them for the next day's journey toward Paulet Island. The dark silhouette of the *Endurance,* broken but still floating, loomed above them as the sleek forms of whales surfaced and resurfaced all around, as if paying their respects to the fallen hero.

They set off the next day with high hopes, but their good spirits were soon dampened. The ice was very uneven and full of obstructions. It was almost impossible, even with the dogs to help, to drag the boats and sledges over it. With the sun high in the sky, the snow covering the ice floes turned to wet, cold mush, and the men and dogs sank into it as they pulled their burdens behind them. They constantly encountered walls of ice several feet high, and since they could not pull their belongings over,

Dragging the lifeboats over the ice was not easy work. They were extremely heavy, and the ice was covered with obstructions.

they were required to skirt around the ice walls until they could find a way through. By the end of the day, after hours of backbreaking effort, they were only one mile closer to Paulet Island. At this rate, it would take them a year to reach land. This was time that they did not have.

Reluctantly, Shackleton told his men that it was no good trying to make for land. The best course of action would be to find a large and stable ice floe, set up a permanent camp, and let the movement of the pack ice do their traveling for them. It would involve weeks, possibly months, of waiting, but the moving ice should eventually bring them within sailing distance of land.

The men were disappointed, but they had seen for themselves that traveling over the ice on foot was close to impossible. Shackleton located a suitable ice floe, and the crew followed him there. The men looked around at his choice: a flat, wide floe more than one-half mile in length. It was just a speck on the frozen sea—an ice desert of white on white, devoid of any life but their own. They named it Ocean Camp, and made it their home.

Frank Wild, second in command of the expedition, and Shackleton (right) examine the conditions of the ice.

CHAPTER SIX

Farewell, *Endurance*

TENTS WERE PITCHED, KENNELS WERE BUILT, AND A makeshift cooking area was constructed. One of the men built a large stove using pieces of metal he had salvaged from the *Endurance*. It was to be rough going, at best. The tents were pitched directly on the ice, and sleeping bags were barely sufficient protection from the cold night air. It was impossible to enter a tent without tracking in snow or slush, and as a result no sleeping bag could remain completely dry.

From Ocean Camp, the wreck of the *Endurance* was clearly visible one and a half miles in the distance. Each day they made numerous trips back over the ice to their ship's remains. Though in pieces, and swamped with water, the vessel was not yet fully submerged. This allowed the men to recover additional supplies, personal possessions, and stores of food. It was a dangerous thing to venture below deck, hip deep in water, to retrieve supplies. The deck was very unstable, and the entire vessel could have dropped below the ice at any time. But when the haul included cases of vegetables, fuel, and clothing, it seemed well worth the risk. Most men kept diaries during the journey, and these were a popular item to retrieve, along with any books that were not waterlogged, providing precious reading material for the stranded crew.

From the vantage point of history, perhaps the most important
things salvaged from the *Endurance* were the negatives belonging to the
ship's photographer, Frank Hurley. On an expedition to little-explored
parts of the world, it was important to have an artist or photographer
along to record the journey. In addition to the scientific and historical
importance of the photographs, they would provide an important
source of income when the expedition was completed. Photos were sold
to newspapers and magazines and used as slides to illustrate the lecture
tours that the expedition members would make. Well before the age of

Ocean Camp.

television, these lecture tours were as close as most of the world would ever come to experiencing the mysteries of the Antarctic, and they were very popular.

The negatives, which were on flat pieces of glass, had been left behind when the *Endurance* was first abandoned. Now, with the luxury of time on his side, Hurley returned for them. The ship's carpenter broke a hole in the side of the ship, and the two men waded below deck and recovered the boxes of negatives, which had been safely sealed. Later, Hurley and Shackleton went through all the negatives and chose a small number to keep with the expedition as they made for land. The remaining negatives were deliberately broken and left in the snow, so that Hurley would not be tempted to save more than he could easily carry. Hurley continued to take pictures throughout their ordeal, and the negative plates that exist today tell their own story of what the men endured.

Enough food was recovered to last the twenty-eight men three months. Since it was quite possible that they would not be rescued in that time, Shackleton sent out hunting parties each day to kill as many seals and penguins as possible. The men had guns, makeshift clubs, knives, and axes with which to do the job. Seals were particularly valuable animals to the castaways, because in addition to providing meat, their thick layer of fat, called blubber, could be used as fuel. Almost every meal that was cooked on the ice was cooked over a seal-blubber fire, and though seal steaks and penguin stew were not especially tasty, the men soon became used to them.

A raised platform was constructed, using planks of wood torn up from the *Endurance*'s decks. The platform served as a lookout tower for the watchman on duty. Though no one expected that any ships would pass within view, the tower did help the men check ice conditions and spot seals and penguins in the distance. Equally important, perhaps, it gave them something to do.

Of everything that had been asked of them so far, doing nothing may have been the hardest. The men had spent a darkened winter in close quarters. The same faces, same songs, same card games, began to grow monotonous. Always eager to have entertainment at hand, Shackleton had one of his men retrieve from the *Endurance* a banjo belonging to Leonard Hussey, the ship's meteorologist. Before long, though, the men grew weary of the sound of the scientist plucking out the same tunes on the damp instrument.

Shackleton (*right*) and Wild (*center*) in front of the lookout tower at Ocean Camp. The man to the left of Wild may be Captain Worsley.

Frank Wild and the wreck of the *Endurance*. Not long after this photo was taken, the ship finally sank.

The days and weeks melted into one another, but the evening of November 21 stuck fast in the memory of each man. As most of them were settling into their sleeping bags for the evening, they heard Sir Ernest calling out to them. They joined him on the floe and watched as the bow of the great *Endurance* dived down below the ice, and the last torn remains of the ship were swallowed up by the sea. Now they were truly alone.

Later, in his journal, Shackleton recorded the ship's passing, and his own anguish, with the words "I cannot write about it."

CHAPTER SEVEN

Life at Ocean Camp

Their plan was now to stay at Ocean Camp until the pack ice began to break up and become looser. Every day, several men would make short trips over the ice to hunt and to look for signs of open water. These excursions were treacherous at best. Floes lay tumbled and overlapping each other. Icy surfaces often gave way and could plunge a man several feet into the frigid water. Shackleton hated to take unnecessary risks, but these frequent hunting and scouting tours were crucial. Conditions were wildly unpredictable, and it was always possible that a freak current or sudden change of wind might open up a lane of water, through which they could make their escape. Because such an escape route might disappear as quickly and unexpectedly as it had appeared, Shackleton prepared the men to be ready at all times. At a moment's notice, they would be able to take down their tents, pack up their belongings, and take to the boats. But days passed, and weeks, and a month, and still the moment did not come.

So they waited. It must have been difficult adapting to this utterly new way of living. Deprived of so many of life's necessities, they found that other things became important. They concentrated all of their energy on hunting, keeping fit, maintaining their equipment, and

Shackleton *(left)* and Wild pose with the rest of the crew at Ocean Camp.

perhaps most important, remaining on good terms with one another. Shackleton was not the only one who understood how crucial it was that the men remain content, relatively cheerful, and without resentment. In their circumstances, even one embittered, dissatisfied man was a great danger. Just as one bad apple can spoil the whole bunch, inevitably the rot would spread to others. Without appearing to do so, Shackleton kept a close watch on the group. The tent assignments he ordered, apparently random, were actually the result of careful thought. Although none of the men were actively rebelling, there were several who were not bearing up as well as others. Shackleton took care to assign these men to his own tent, where his powerful influence would overcome their gloomy attitudes.

They were a mixed group of officers, experienced sailors, scientists, and adventurers. While Shackleton was the leader of the overall expedition, the ship's captain, Frank Worsley, had commanded the day-to-day operation of the *Endurance*. A native of New Zealand, Worsley had made his living on the sea since his mid-teens. In addition to his capabilities as ship's captain, Worsley was a brilliant navigator. In circumstances during which absolutely precise navigation meant the difference between life and death, his talents made him an invaluable addition to the expedition. He was handsome and spirited, and his expertise, liveliness, and unfailing good humor endeared him to Shackleton. Another man on whom Sir Ernest would come to rely heavily was Frank Wild, second in command of the expedition. Shackleton first met Wild on Scott's 1901 Antarctic expedition. They became good friends, and Wild accompanied Shackleton on every succeeding trip he made to the southern continent. Small in stature, he had the strength and endurance of a great man. There seemed to be no hardship or extreme temperature he could not happily withstand. No land was too distant, no adventure too dangerous. Highly intelligent and goodhearted, energetic and courageous almost to a fault, he and Shackleton seemed cut from the same cloth.

Frank Wild, second in command of the expedition.

Frank Hurley, expedition photographer.

Frank Hurley was an Australian photographer responsible for documenting the expedition on film. Like so many others who had joined with Shackleton, he was a seasoned risk taker with a taste for unknown adventure. It was not uncommon to spot Hurley high up the mast, legs wound around a slender yardarm, his sizable camera and tripod perched precariously before him as the ship pitched and tossed in the waves. Hurley was also extremely resourceful, fashioning cooking devices, pumps, and other small inventions from bits of wood and metal he had pulled from the ruined ship.

Percy Blackborrow, an eager, nineteen-year-old sailor from Wales, had made his best efforts to win a place on Shackleton's expedition, but there were no positions left open. His disappointment was so sharp that he was inspired to hide himself in one of the ship's lockers before departure. The stowaway was discovered by a crewman when they had been several days at sea. Shackleton pretended to be enraged, shouting at the shaking boy in thunderous tones. It was only when Shackleton shouted that if they ran out of food, they would have to eat the young Welshman, that Blackborrow realized the humorous Irishman was more amused than angry. Blackborrow was given a job helping the cook, and if the crew's youngest member later came to regret his decision to sneak aboard the ill-fated *Endurance,* he never showed those feelings.

At the age of fifty-six, Harry McNeish, ship's carpenter, was the oldest man on the voyage. McNeish was a masterful woodworker, and

Shackleton relied on his talents to reinforce the lifeboats, adapt and maintain the sledges, and construct shelters for the cooking and supply areas. Though skilled in his craft, McNeish was somewhat lacking in the social graces. He tended to keep to himself and could be humorless at times. He was one of the men whom Shackleton watched closely for any signs of impending trouble.

These and other faces made up the population of lonely Ocean Camp, which Worsley thought resembled a small cluster of tepees. The men continued to exercise and game, gambling with imaginary holdings and winning and losing pretend fortunes in a matter of hours. Shackleton launched a message in a bottle, explaining what had happened to the *Endurance* and advising that all was well. The bottle and its message were never recovered and may well be there to this day, bobbing among the waves or entombed within an ice floe.

Between what they caught and what they salvaged from the *Endurance*, there was still enough food to keep each man satisfied. In addition to seal and penguin, the main ingredients of their diet were hot drinks—such as tea, powdered milk, and cocoa—dried vegetables, biscuits and bread, and hoosh. Hoosh was their word for a paste of concentrated meat and vegetables that was mixed with boiling water, creating a satisfying hot stew. These meals were all prepared by Charles Green, the cook, who often worked nonstop, even in the worst weather conditions, to ensure that the men had hot refreshments. It took some time before cooking in these conditions was perfected; in fact their small supply of Irish stew was lost when the stove collapsed, dumping the precious food onto the wooden embers. This did not discourage some of the men, who simply nibbled the stew off the cooling embers as if they were eating corn on the cob. In time, Green became an expert, easily preparing meals for twenty-eight during the worst of blizzards.

By December, Captain Worsley calculated that they had gained more than one hundred miles since they had abandoned their ship. Blizzards, though they caused some discomfort, were welcomed because they generally caused the ice pack to travel much faster. With each storm, the men were swept miles closer to land, but their progress was hard won. The constant assault by wind and snow had taken its toll on Ocean Camp. The battered floe was becoming smaller and smaller, and the once firm ice was beginning to show signs of stress.

In late December, after allowing a small feast of specially saved rations including sausages, ham, baked beans, and peaches, Shackleton ordered the sledges packed up. Ocean Camp was disintegrating beneath their feet, and he no longer considered it safe. It was time, he told them, to be on the move.

CHAPTER EIGHT

On the Move

Each evening before marching, Shackleton and Wild set out to scout the best and safest route, marking it with flags so it could be easily followed. Because the sun now turned much of the ice-covered snow to mush during the daylight hours, the men traveled during the short nights and slept during the day. It was brutally hard work, but the men were so happy to be on the move after eight weeks of inactivity at Ocean Camp that they scarcely minded.

Only a few days into the march, however, they encountered the same problems they had experienced during the first march for Paulet Island. Their path was often obstructed by huge pressure ridges, or walls of ice, that they had to climb over. Even at night, the snow covering the ice pack was soft, and the men, dogs, and sledges sank into it as they pulled. Because both men and dogs were working so hard, they needed much more to eat than they had at Ocean Camp. Checking over their stores, Shackleton knew there was not enough food to get them to Paulet Island under these conditions. In a week of grueling effort, they had made just over seven miles' progress. Clearly, they could not go forward, and because the ice pack behind them was unstable, they could not go back. Once again they were stuck and at the mercy of the ice.

The same twenty-five-foot-high ice slab that helped block the progress of the sleds made a good look-out point.

Shackleton located the largest and sturdiest floe within view, and the dejected group unpacked their sledges and pitched their tents. It was obvious that there would be no more marching. They could not move now until the sun, wind, and current provided enough open ocean for them to escape by boat. The last teams of dogs were shot, and the men settled into their second home on ice, appropriately named Patience Camp.

Their supplies of food were dwindling each day, and they set about hunting to lay in a fresh supply of meat. In addition to providing much needed nourishment, the meals of fresh meat did something the dry supplies and hoosh could not. The meat protected the men from scurvy, the most dreaded disease of sailors and explorers. Although some important clues had been discovered as to the cause of scurvy, in Shackleton's day it was still not precisely known what caused the disease, which weakened microscopic blood vessels and caused symptoms ranging from bleeding and loss of teeth to complete physical and mental breakdown. If untreated, scurvy eventually killed its victims. It is now known that scurvy is a dietary disorder caused by lack of vitamin C, which is found in fresh fruits, vegetables, and some meats. Had the crew of the *Endurance* not had access to the fresh meat provided by seals and penguins, they would have certainly succumbed to scurvy long before reaching Patience Camp.

Though the food supply was rapidly diminishing, Sir Ernest often produced a special treat he had hidden away, such as a small supply of onions to be fried up with breakfast. During their months stranded on the ice, the men could not help but notice that Shackleton never allowed himself any of the special privileges to which he was entitled as expedition leader. His rations were exactly the same as that allowed the lowest rank of sailor, he took his equal (or greater) share of work and watch duty, and he shared his tent with several other men, rather than keeping his lodgings private. He gave his good boots to a man who needed them

Hurley and Shackleton with Patience Camp's makeshift stove. Hurley, seen here skinning a seal, built the stove himself from bits and pieces he salvaged from the wreck of the *Endurance*.

and his mittens to another who lost his own in the ocean. It was by behavior such as this that Shackleton inspired such fierce and lifelong loyalty among his men. They felt beyond a shadow of a doubt that he would die for them if necessary, and this inspired in them a desire to give him their very best efforts at all times. Every last crew member knew that Shackleton had never lost a life on any expedition he had led. This knowledge, and Shackleton's own example, continued to inspire them as they waited at Patience Camp with little food, and little time, left to them.

It was now March. They had been at Patience Camp since January 1, and they could only pray that the pack ice would open up so that they could take to the boats before they were swept past land altogether. The Antarctic continent extends in an armlike length of land now called the Antarctic Peninsula. Beyond this peninsula lie several groups of islands,

An igloo-kitchen at Patience Camp.

Preparing dinner.

which are the last land to be found before the open ocean. Because of the fierce wind and ocean currents, it would be quite impossible to sail or row the small lifeboats back to these islands, or to the Palmer Peninsula, once the pack ice had carried the group past. Captain Worsley frequently took readings to determine their position and to see what land they might hope to intersect. By this time, judging from their course, Worsley felt fairly certain that they would drift past Paulet Island. They could no longer hope to reach the food and supplies that had been stored there.

A strange mix of boredom and apprehension settled over the men. They could do nothing but wait, knowing that if the pack carried them out into the open ocean, Patience Camp would be destroyed by the great waves. Though it was not obvious to his men, Shackleton's anxiety was growing. He constantly had dreams of accidents befalling his men, and at night Hurley, one of his tentmates, would often awaken to hear Shackleton crying out in the grip of a nightmare.

One dreadful day in late March they actually caught sight of land. The ice surrounding Patience Camp was impassable by foot, but still too thick to launch the boats through. Not knowing if they would come across any more land, they helplessly drifted on until the stretch of coast disappeared from sight.

By the captain's calculations, the men had now passed the tip of the Palmer Peninsula, and their only hope was to make for one of two destinations: Elephant Island or Clarence Island. If they were unable to reach one of these islands, which they were now approaching, they would continue on into the violent open sea, where they had virtually no chance of survival.

By the beginning of April, nature forced them into action. The floe making up Patience Camp had cracked repeatedly and been reduced in size from one mile to just more than two hundred yards in diameter. The smaller it got, the more the ocean below tossed it about. This in turn caused more breaks, and the floe grew even smaller. Men were employed at all times to watch the ice, so that the group would have warning when a new crack appeared. The ice beyond Patience Camp, once tightly formed in large floes, had now been chopped and battered into small, soft pieces. When, on April 9, the floe again split in two directly below their camp, Shackleton knew they could delay no longer. There was a small alley beyond the floe that was somewhat free of ice. Though it was by no means an ideal or safe route, it was preferable to remaining on Patience Camp, where they were likely to be dropped into the freezing ocean at any moment. Clarence and Elephant Islands lay, by the captain's estimation, some sixty miles away. Shackleton ordered the camp struck and stowed, and they lowered their three boats into the water and began to row for land.

CHAPTER NINE

"The Worst Sea in the World"

THE MEN SCARCELY HAD TIME TO ADJUST THEMSELVES to the boats when they heard a strange noise, as if a train were approaching. They turned in the direction of the noise and could barely believe their eyes. A wall of large pack-ice fragments, perched atop the crest of a rapidly advancing wave, was threatening to overtake and swamp the three small boats. A freak current had created a wave of ice that raged over the sea like a stampeding rhinoceros. Heeding Shackleton's urgent shouts, the men pulled the oars and rowed with all their might. The three boats were directly in the ice wave's path, and their only option was to try to outrun it.

For nearly a quarter of an hour, the wave continued to pursue them. Then suddenly, as quickly as it had appeared, it sank back into the ocean like a mythical sea monster and disappeared altogether. They had raced the ice and won.

Icy tidal waves were only one of the hazards the men faced in the water. Few animals could survive in the frigid Weddell Sea, but the waters were home to one of the world's most deadly mammals—the killer whale. Measuring up to thirty feet long and weighing over eight tons, the killer whale is armed with dozens of razor-sharp teeth and is an aggressive and ferocious hunter. The killers were constantly surfacing all around the three boats, which each measured just over twenty feet long. Should one of these monsters come up for air directly beneath one of the boats, the boat would capsize and its crew would be killed, if not by drowning then by the teeth of the whale.

Another constant threat was the large chunks of ice floating everywhere. Until the boats pulled free of the loose pack ice, there was always the possibility that they would be struck and sunk by one of these pack fragments, or squashed between two colliding chunks. These demolition-derby conditions made navigation very difficult, but it was crucial that Captain Worsley correctly calculate their position and course. They still suffered the risk of missing the islands, and even a small navigational error could cause them to miss their target altogether. The three boats stuck close together—Worsley captaining the *Dudley Docker*, Shackleton in command of the *James Caird*, and Hubert Hudson, the navigation officer, at the helm of the *Stancomb Wills*.

Night came quickly, for there were now seventeen hours of darkness each day. Sir Ernest decided that they should make camp on a small ice floe for the night, before pushing on for the islands in the morning.

After a quick meal of seal meat, the men took to their tents. Shackleton was snugly settled in his sleeping bag, tired from the day's rowing, when he was gripped by a feeling that something was not right. He left his tent and began to walk over the ice to alert the night watchman to possible danger. As he passed one of the crew's tents, he was horrified to see it stretch across the ice, as the floe beneath it drew apart in two pieces. Stunned and sleepy men tumbled from the tent as Shackleton cried out to them, but one was not quick enough. As the ice opened up, the man plunged into the freezing black water. Shackleton lunged forward, ripped away the fallen tent, and thrust his arm blindly into the water. With one massive gesture he plucked the man, still trapped in his soaking sleeping bag, out of the ocean. As the man lay shivering on the floe, the two pieces of ice came together again, and the pool from which he had been rescued disappeared.

Shaken by the close call, all of the men were awakened, counted, and directed to move the supplies to the largest and steadiest remaining portion of the floe. With all hands helping, the supplies and men were soon safely on the steady floe. Shackleton, who had remained on the smaller ice fragment to supervise the transfer of stores, then attempted to join his men, but he floated out of reach and into the black of night. A boat was hastily launched, and it was only by following the sound of his voice that his men were able to find him in the dark and bring him back to the floe.

RICK PRICE/CORBIS

Although it lacks the huge waves that were often present on the Weddell Sea, this contemporary photograph, with pack fragments in the foreground and bergs in the rear, gives some idea of the kind of conditions the three boats would have encountered.

There was no more sleep for the crew that night. They waited until the first hint of light appeared on the horizon, then resumed their boat journey for land. Little progress was made. Stormy seas, the curse of the Antarctic, again overtook them. The little boats struggled through the growing waves. Shackleton was hesitant to order the men back onto the ice given the previous night's drama, but the fierce winds and choppy seas made conditions in the boats extremely unsafe. Rather than returning to an ice floe, however, Shackleton decided that they would make for a nearby iceberg, ninety feet long and rising twenty feet out of the water. On top of this presumably solid ice fortress, the men took refuge and waited out the night for the heavy seas to subside. Instead, the weather grew worse.

Perched high atop the berg, the men got some badly needed sleep. But on waking, they saw that the swell of the ocean had become uncommonly high, battering their berg with truck-size pieces of ice. With each onslaught, another large chunk of the berg was torn off and swallowed by the waves. An old pattern was repeating itself; the swell had packed ice fragments neatly around their berg. The fragments were too small to climb onto, and too large to get the boats through. The men waited tensely as the berg continued to disintegrate beneath their feet. It was obvious to all that it was no good. From their elevated position on top of the iceberg, it was clear that the broken pack ice extended far into the distance. As resourceful, strong, and courageous as Shackleton was, he could not move mountains. What happened next could not be explained.

The ice fragments surrounding the berg began to part before their eyes. It was as if an invisible hand had descended into the sea and was sweeping clear a path. With no time to organize, Shackleton shouted to the men to throw the boats into the water and toss the supplies in after them. They leaped into the boats and sped through the mysteriously ice-free lane, until they reached safer waters.

The Weddell Sea is unpredictable and complicated, and no one completely understands the strange currents and tides that lie within it. Certainly stranger things had happened than the sudden appearance of clear water. But this was not the first time events had conspired to save them just as it seemed all was lost, and it would not be the last. Some began to feel what they called the hand of Providence guiding them. Or perhaps it was just good luck. Whatever the explanation, it was a considerably thankful crew of men who resumed the struggle for land.

After their second close call on the ice, Shackleton resolved that they should sleep in the boats from that time forward. This was their third day in the boats, and it was marked by heavy weather and large waves. By dusk, the men were soaked to the skin and utterly exhausted. They could barely see through the wind-whipped snow and spray and had to call out constantly to one another to avoid becoming separated from the other boats. Through the night, they continually heard the loud explosions of hissing air that indicated the presence of a killer whale surfacing. It was their longest night so far, but the men felt their strength returning with the sunrise.

Confident that the hardships they endured would be rewarded by the progress made, Shackleton eagerly awaited Worsley's calculations of the distance they had covered. A disbelieving Shackleton looked blackly at the captain. Worsley's readings showed that the seas and wind had swept them back thirty miles. Not only had they made absolutely no progress, they had actually lost some distance. They were now farther from land than they had been when they departed Patience Camp three days earlier. Devastated, Shackleton told his crew only that they had not made as much distance as he would have liked.

By the following day, April 13, they had passed out of the pack ice and were in clear waters. By this time, based on Worsley's calculations, they had decided that Elephant Island would be their destination. From their new position, it lay almost one hundred miles in the distance. Temperatures continued to drop, and the only relief was rowing, which was hard work but served to keep the men warm. Their beards and mustaches froze white, and they looked like living statues.

They alternately rowed, sailed, and slept as night turned to day and back to night again. Because they were out of the pack ice, they had much larger waves with which to contend. Their soaked shoes and clothing literally froze around them. They were making progress now, but thirst and hunger coupled with frostbite and exhaustion ate away at them. With no pack ice to melt, they had lost their only source of fresh water, and it grew increasingly difficult to row, or even to eat, in the face of their growing thirst. Some chewed raw seal meat, hoping the bloody animal flesh would help to ease their thirst.

On April 14, their sixth day in the boats, Elephant Island loomed into view in the distance. Captain Worsley's navigation had been flawless, and Shackleton congratulated him. Neither Worsley, Wild, or Shackleton had slept during the last three days and nights, and they could not sleep now. It would be at least one more day before they would reach land, and they were far from safe. The men could see the coastline clearly, but as they raced for the shore, the wind and waves again began to rage.

They struggled all day, with wind, ice, and current combining to prevent them from approaching the shore. Waves swamped the three boats as the daylight began to fail. They would not make landfall that day and did not have the strength to last another. The three boats waited out the night in the clutches of the gale, fighting to maintain their positions. An exhausted Worsley finally dropped off to sleep at the tiller of his boat, the *Dudley Docker*. Unable to keep the boat on course, one of his men tried to awaken him, but he lay cold and still. They believed he was dead, until one of them finally managed to rouse him by kicking him sharply in the head.

After what must have seemed an eternity, the first faint light of dawn crept over them, and the heavy seas relented. The coast of Elephant Island lay directly ahead, easily within reach. The gale delivered bits of glacier, which floated abundantly around them, solving the very immediate danger that they might die of thirst.

At Shackleton's direction, they began to pull for shore as the sun more fully lit the scene. But as he looked about, Shackleton saw only one other boat. The *Dudley Docker* and her crew, with Captain Worsley at the helm, had vanished without a trace.

CHAPTER TEN

Solid Ground Underfoot

Shackleton shouted his orders as the two boats struggled toward a small beach. He prepared to give the order to land, timing it carefully as so not to be dashed on the rocks by the waves. It was at this moment that he glanced over the rocky coast and was stunned and delighted to see the *Dudley Docker* coming around the point, making straight for them. Worsley had also feared for the safety of the other boats when he did not see them at first light. Hoping they had simply been blown in different directions in the darkness of night, Worsley had skirted the island's coast until he caught sight of other boats in the distance. The two groups greeted each other with shouts and cheers, and it was a complete party of three boats and twenty-eight men that finally pulled onto the shore of Elephant Island.

It had been almost six months since they had abandoned the *Endurance* and well over a year since the men had felt the earth beneath their feet. During their first few minutes ashore, the gloomy and barren beach seemed as luxurious and inviting a piece of real estate as the men had ever visited. They staggered around like drunken sailors on shore leave, scooping up handfuls of blackened pebbles and jubilantly running their fingers over them as if they were made of gold.

Landing on Elephant
Island.

With some effort, the boats and supplies were hauled high onto the
rocks to avoid the possibility that a wave would sweep their belongings
out to sea. An elephant seal was spotted and killed, and from it the cook
made a hot and satisfying stew. Their strength and spirits returning, the
men tried to grow accustomed to the sensation of solid ground underfoot. Worsley described the bemused crew as wandering about like a
band of "harmless lunatics."

Shackleton knew that most of the men were truly exhausted, and more than one of them faced failing health. Blackborrow, the stowaway, was suffering from frostbitten feet, which caused the young Welshman much distress. There was still a lot to be done, but it could wait. Sir Ernest ordered that each man eat as much of the cook's hot stew as he wanted. The men eagerly followed orders, then collapsed into sleep inside their hastily pitched tents.

Shackleton took advantage of this time to examine their little beach with the help of Worsley, Wild, and Hurley. It was obvious from the state of the beach that their campsite would not always be protected

It is believed Shackleton and his crew were the first men ever to set foot on the island.

The men's first meal after landing. Shackleton is in profile, fourth from right.

from the tides. The rocks showed evidence that the area frequently found itself underwater. In addition, there was no shelter from the raging wind, so they were in constant danger of being flooded or blown away at the first approach of a storm. The four men agreed; they would have to move to a safer spot on the island. They could manage for a day or two, but afterward, it would be back to the boats.

The gale that had made landing on the island so difficult continued to blow, but nothing could prevent the men from enjoying precious sleep. Shackleton, Worsley, and Wild, who had gone virtually without rest for the better part of a week, all slept eighteen straight hours.

The following day, the men spread their soaked belongings all over the little beach to dry. Wild set out in one of the boats to scout for a more protected campsite. Looking over his men, Shackleton could see too well the toll the last six months had taken on them. The stout Irishman himself had not escaped the physical effects of their ordeal. Worsley found that Shackleton looked years older than he had that December day when he first boarded the *Endurance* with high hopes and powerful spirits.

Wild sailed up and down the coast in the *Stancomb Wills* but discovered only one suitable area that seemed somewhat protected from wind and water. He returned to camp and reported his findings to Shackleton, who immediately ordered all hands to stow their supplies, for they would move the next morning. The men alternately slept and hunched around the campfire, eating elephant-seal steaks and bemoaning the ill fortune that would force them back onto the hated sea.

The next morning, April 17, it was an extremely unenthusiastic crew who climbed back into the three boats from which they had so recently escaped. The new campsite lay about eight miles down the island's coast. There didn't seem to be any calm weather to be had on Elephant Island, and the wind picked up as they launched the boats. It was difficult starting off, as the incoming waves kept sweeping the boats back onshore. During the launch, three of their oars were broken, which was a decidedly bad turn of luck.

Once clear of the shore, they almost immediately encountered high winds, and visibility was poor because of the flying pillars of sea spray, which they called willy-waws. Rowing through these conditions required a fierce effort, and two more oars were broken in the process. In Captain Worsley's *Dudley Docker*, only three unbroken oars remained, and the *Docker* soon fell behind the other two boats. Captain Worsley and his crew had no choice but to struggle on, rowing twice as hard to compensate for the lost oars. The wind was constantly changing direction, so they could not hoist their sail for fear of being capsized by a sudden wind shift.

The *Caird* and the *Stancomb Wills* surged ahead, but the *Docker*, lagging behind for lack of rowing power, had to take shelter behind a large rock and wait for the wind to die down. Three hours later, the wind dropped off, and they began to pull again for land. In the distance, they could see the *Stancomb Wills* and the *James Caird* already ashore. A half hour after leaving the rock, the *Docker* limped in to join them.

At first glance their new campsite did not seem much of an improvement. The beach, if the rocky mess underfoot could be described as such, was thoroughly wet. Though larger and more removed from the tide, it offered virtually no protection from the vicious wind tearing over the island. However, there was no discussion of moving again. Wild had said this was the only area that could accommodate their group, and Shackleton knew Wild was as good as his word. And some of the men were growing increasingly weak. Blackborrow, nursing his frostbitten feet, was unable to get out of the boat without help. Another sailor, Louis Rickinson, had suffered a heart attack, and a third seaman showed signs of mental instability. There were two doctors in the group, and the patients were well cared for and out of immediate danger, but they were invalids nonetheless. Other men suffered from physical exhaustion, exposure to the cold, mental stress, or all three.

The wind screamed all around them on their first night at Cape Wild, which Shackleton had named for its discoverer, but the weary men scarcely noticed. They were so tired that when Worsley's tent was ripped into pieces by the wind, the men inside simply pulled the remaining shreds of canvas on top of them like a blanket and snuggled more deeply into their sleeping bags.

The next morning, which began their first full day at Cape Wild, they realized that the violent blowing was a constant and unchanging feature of their location. The wind was so strong it blew Shackleton to the ground as he was hunting a seal. Ice fragments the size of dinner plates blew through the air, making even a brief walk down the beach a dangerous expedition.

Winter was fast approaching, and there was no guarantee that their food supplies would see them through it. They still hunted for seals and penguins but did not know how long the supply would hold out. It was extremely unlikely that help would ever find them. They would have to find the help themselves.

It was time for Shackleton to go.

CHAPTER ELEVEN

A Crew Divided

THERE WAS NEVER MUCH DOUBT AS TO WHERE SHACKLETON had to go. Though Tierra del Fuego and the Falkland Islands, some five hundred miles away, were the closest pockets of civilization, the winds and currents moved in the opposite direction, making reaching them practically impossible. His only hope was to make for the island of South Georgia, which lay to the northeast. Shackleton knew that its whaling stations would be peopled with sailors, and that he might find a vessel there capable of returning to Elephant Island to rescue his crew. All he needed to do was to pilot a small, open lifeboat eight hundred miles through the world's most violent and storm-rocked ocean. It was a challenge Sir Ernest rose to without hesitation.

Captain Worsley was perhaps the person who best understood the dangers involved in the journey, and the large margin for failure. As an experienced sailor and the most talented navigator among them, Worsley knew that at this latitude at the bottom of the world, the earth's rotation causes the dominant winds to blow from the west to the east. These winds, called the prevailing westerlies, drive the ocean currents in the same eastward direction. With no significant blocks of land to slow them, the wind and currents stampede through the wide avenue between the tip of South America and Antarctica. Known as the Drake Passage, this area of ocean is a lethal brew of monstrous waves and constant gales.

Shackleton would need a crew of five men to assist him on the voyage. Almost all of the men who were able volunteered, and after careful deliberation, Sir Ernest made his choices. He could not do without the navigational talents of Captain Worsley or the services of the carpenter, McNeish, to maintain the boat on what would be a rough trip. He also chose three seasoned and hearty sailors, Tom Crean, a fellow Irishman, John Vincent, and Tim McCarthy. All of these sailors were old hands on a ship, and all had spent most of their adult lives at sea. His old companion Wild was disappointed not to be chosen, but Shackleton relied on him to keep things under control on Elephant Island in his absence. Once they had departed, Wild would be the official leader of the remaining men.

The *James Caird* was the largest and most seaworthy of the three lifeboats, though at just over twenty-two feet long it hardly seemed big enough to weather the journey. Using wood salvaged from the other two boats, they had already added to the *Caird*'s sides, to make them higher. This would be of some help in withstanding the great waves they would encounter. They filled the seams between the planks of wood with a paste made of seal blood and oil paints borrowed from George Marston, the ship's artist. The best parts of the remaining boats were also salvaged to make the *Caird* as seaworthy as possible. They used one of the masts to reinforce the *Caird*'s hull, placing it lengthwise in the boat so that it acted as a kind of spine. The carpenter then covered much of the boat in old tent canvas, which would provide an enclosed area beneath which the men could sleep.

Large stones were loaded into the bottom of the boat to act as ballast, a heavy material meant to improve the boat's stability. With this extra

Reinforcing the *Caird* in preparation for Shackleton's departure.

weight, the *Caird* would gain badly needed defense against capsizing. Feeling the journey should not take much more than two weeks, Shackleton packed thirty days' worth of supplies, including cases of food and powdered milk, and fresh water melted from the glacier that loomed over Cape Wild. They also brought two makeshift stoves, a good supply of matches and candles, and six sleeping bags. Worsley had managed to keep some of his navigation charts and instruments undamaged, and he packed these carefully below the canvas deck.

All hands somberly helped the six men prepare for their departure. Many of them privately feared they would never see Shackleton again. Frank Hurley went so far as to prepare a document for Shackleton's signature, giving Hurley all reproduction and publishing rights to his photographs in the event of Shackleton's death. Shackleton signed it without comment.

On April 24, all was finally ready, and the *Caird* and her crew of six set off, waving at their companions until the waves hid them from view. If all went well, they would be rescued in perhaps a month's time. It was

Launching the *Caird* on her rescue mission.

a long shot, but the men trusted Shackleton, and they knew that if the voyage could be made, he was the man to make it.

With the *Caird* now out of sight, Wild turned his attention to their camp. Unable to dig an ice cave, the men created a shelter from two overturned boats. Their new home measured only nineteen feet long and ten feet wide. Inside, the roof was just five feet from the ground, making it impossible to stand upright. What canvas had not been used on the *Caird* was used for walls and a rough carpet, and blankets hung over the door to keep out the wind and snow. The canvas walls were reinforced with hard-packed snow, but nothing kept the elements out altogether. Still, it was the best they could do, and at times it seemed almost cozy. Some warmth was generated from the cooking stove, which was placed inside the shelter. A chimney made of tin directed most of the smoke outside. The men rotated their dining positions daily, so that each man got to spend some time in the highly prized spot nearest the stove.

The canvas and snow walls beneath the boats let in no light, so Wild cut several holes in the canvas, and inserted some glass lids

The makeshift hut made of two overturned lifeboats.

An early unsuccessful attempt to dig an ice cave on Elephant Island.

taken from the ship's instruments. These improvised windows, four in all, allowed the grateful men to relieve their boredom by reading or playing cards. Six precious books had survived, including some poetry and several volumes of the encyclopedia. Next to food, these were among the most sought-after items on all of Elephant Island. Many of the men were also keeping diaries. These journals provide an un-equaled source of information, more precious even than Hurley's photographs. They tell of dreams, emotions, smells, and sounds that the photographs could not capture. Many still exist, some in family collections and some in museums.

The men settled into a routine of hunting for food, making repairs to the shelter, and performing the tasks of cooking and fire tending. All the while they scanned the seas in the hope of glimpsing a rescue ship. It was a familiar mix of boredom and anxiety in cramped quarters, and tempers occasionally flared. Food was a particular source of quarrels, and it was difficult to avoid friction when an unidentified culprit stole some biscuits from the stores. Still, under Wild's leadership, a sense of calm and order was maintained. Ultimately, each man knew he was no better off than the next. None of them had had a bath in almost ten months, and one man joked in his diary that he took comfort in the thought that it simply wasn't possible to get any dirtier than they already were.

The weather never improved for long. As one month gave way to a second, and a third, the men were confronted with a parade of hurricanes and blizzards. The Antarctic winter had arrived, and temperatures swung from bitterly cold to just above freezing. When the air warmed, floods of melting snow soon followed, requiring the men to bail water tirelessly from their shelter. All things considered, they preferred the cold temperatures, for at least their sleeping bags remained dry.

During this time, the condition of Blackborrow's feet had dangerously worsened. Frostbite was an unavoidable companion of all who braved the extreme cold without adequate protection. Most often affecting the toes, fingers, or nose, frostbite occurs when excessive cold causes the skin to freeze. In severe cases such as Blackborrow's, when circumstances prevented the thawing of the frozen tissue, gangrene set in. Gangrene, which indicates that the frozen skin tissue has died, is a potentially dangerous condition that can spread to other parts of the body. Often the only effective treatment is the removal of the dead skin. For Blackborrow, unhappily, this meant an operation, performed under appalling conditions, to amputate all five of the toes on his foot.

The surgery was performed by the two doctors, James McIlroy and Alexander Macklin, beneath the shelter of the overturned lifeboats. With only candlelight to see by and the air smudged with black smoke from the stove, the two doctors performed the operation as the other men looked on. The operation was a success, and at the cost of his toes and considerable discomfort, Blackborrow kept his legs—and his life.

Wild took his duties as leader very seriously, and he patterned himself after Shackleton, whom he deeply admired. He placed great importance on good morale, as did Shackleton. He worked with Macklin and McIlroy to ensure that the weakest men continued to improve. He continued the Shackleton tradition of scheduling small entertainments to amuse the men. Miraculously, six months after abandoning the *Endurance* and struggling over ice and water, Hussey's banjo was still in one piece. At Wild's direction, Hussey gave a concert once a week, and though the number of songs he knew never increased, the music still cheered the group of grimy castaways.

Sometimes, however, Wild's commitment to Shackleton's style of leadership caused him to act in a shortsighted way. Shackleton, whom Wild called "the Boss," was a firm believer in optimism. This meant proceeding as if the best possible outcome was expected. To give the impression that he fully expected the Boss to return and give rescue any day, Wild refused to gather a huge supply of meat. Enough seals and penguins were hunted to lay in a decent stock, but beyond that Wild prevented further hunting, to avoid the appearance that he anticipated many more months of waiting. Shackleton had made the same decision during their stay on the ice. As the men feared, the seals did eventually migrate away from their beach, and fewer and fewer penguins remained.

The possibility that their supply of meat would run out made the men begin to grow fearful. It was now nearing the end of August, and there was no sign of a rescue. The men were boiling seaweed to eat as the portions of meat grew smaller. Wild began each day by calling, "Lash up and stow, boys, the Boss may come today!" Privately, however, some of the men were beginning to worry. Shackleton and his crew had departed almost four months ago, on a journey that should have taken only several weeks. If Sir Ernest had reached South Georgia, he surely would have moved heaven and earth to get a rescue ship back to Elephant Island. Too much time had passed, and though no one dared voice the thought, more than one man secretly feared Shackleton had never reached his destination—that the Boss and his crew of five were dead.

CHAPTER TWELVE

The Seaworthy *Caird*

The first few hours of the *Caird*'s voyage were smooth sailing indeed. The sun shone, in itself a rarity, and the wind blew briskly. These were ideal conditions. Behind them, the crew could see Elephant Island growing smaller in the distance. From afar, the island looked serene and majestic beneath the cliffs and snow-covered mountains. The men on board the *Caird*, however, knew better.

With Captain Worsley's direction, the *Caird* gingerly picked her way through the loose pack, heading for open sea. Chunks of ice the size of buildings gave the men the impression they were navigating down the main street of a bustling town. To Worsley's fanciful imagination, the ice floating all around them made up a zoo of creatures. He saw giraffes, crocodiles, bears, elephants atop Swiss chalets, and ducks, all icy and white, where others saw only loose pack. Just before sunset, they passed by the last clumps of ice and sailed into free and clear waters. In minutes they had left the ice—their enemy and friend of so many months— behind them.

Late that evening, most of the crew went down to sleep in the little enclosed area beneath the canvas decking. Shackleton and Worsley remained in the open area at the back, or aft, of the boat. It was a rare, clear evening, and the constellations were vivid through the bitterly cold air. Awed by the sprawling beauty overhead, the two friends sat close together for warmth and talked of their futures. It was an evening neither of them would forget—a brief span of quiet companionship in an otherwise tumultuous time.

The good weather continued for the first day and night of their journey, and they made good distance. By the second day, a considerable gale blew up, tossing the *Caird* carelessly about. They plodded on, however, and by April 26, their third day out, they were 128 miles from Elephant Island. They had covered one eighth of the distance to South Georgia in just three days. This provided a badly needed boost to the men, most of whom were feeling a little unwell. After so many months on the ice, they had become unused to the rocking sensation of the open sea, and even Captain Worsley was admitting to a little seasickness.

Even in good weather, conditions onboard the little boat were miserably uncomfortable. The wind blew waves and spray over the *Caird* constantly, and the carefully constructed canvas shelter began to sag under the weight of the freezing water. With the help of a pump built by Hurley, they could bail the water out of the boat, but this could not prevent all of their belongings from getting soaked.

Below the canvas deck was a tumble of the ballast stones, supplies, and sleeping bags. This entire cabin, if it could be called such, measured only seven feet long and five feet wide, and grew narrower toward the bow, or front end, of the boat. The canvas ceiling was barely high enough to allow the men to sit up. It was in this tiny dark hole that the men had to sleep, cook, and eat. With the boat rolling in the waves, the men were alternately tossed against the sharp corners of the food boxes and bounced on the rocks. Under these conditions, it was difficult to get any sleep in the wet, and increasingly slimy, sleeping bags.

They divided into two groups of three men each. When one group

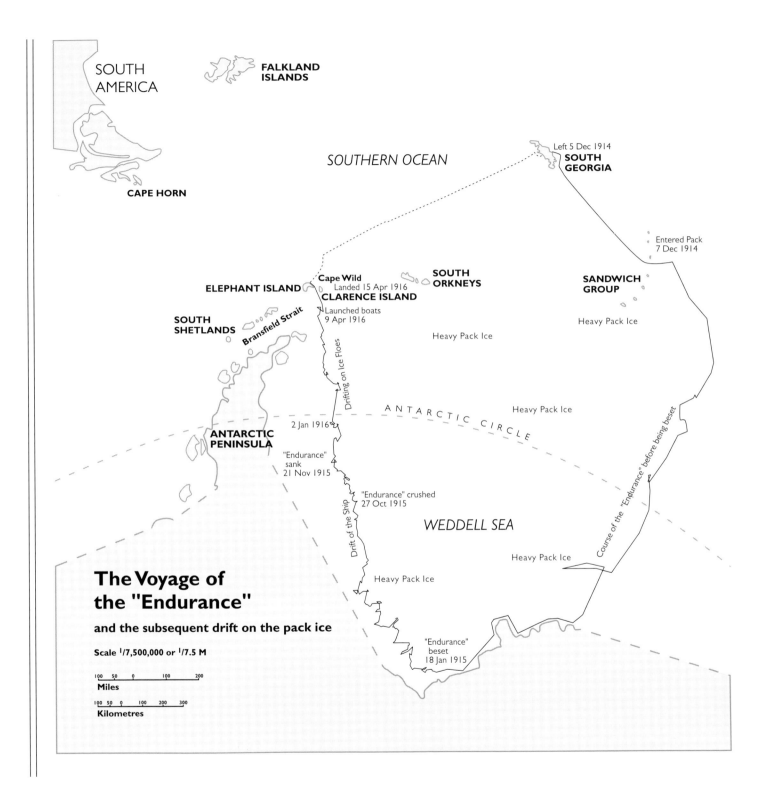

SOUTH
AMERICA

FALKLAND
ISLANDS

CAPE HORN

SOUTHERN OCEAN

Left 5 Dec 1914
SOUTH
GEORGIA

Entered Pack
7 Dec 1914

Cape Wild
Landed 15 Apr 1916
ELEPHANT ISLAND
CLARENCE ISLAND

SOUTH
ORKNEYS

SANDWICH
GROUP

Heavy Pack Ice

SOUTH
SHETLANDS

Bransfield Strait

Launched boats
9 Apr 1916

Drifting on Ice Floes

Heavy Pack Ice

A N T A R C T I C   C I R C L E

Heavy Pack Ice

Course of the "Endurance" before being beset

2 Jan 1916

ANTARCTIC
PENINSULA

"Endurance"
sank
21 Nov 1915

"Endurance" crushed
27 Oct 1915

WEDDELL SEA

Drift of the Ship

Heavy Pack Ice

Heavy Pack Ice

The Voyage of the "Endurance"

and the subsequent drift on the pack ice

Scale 1/7,500,000 or 1/7.5 M

100   50   0   100   200
Miles

100 50 0   100   200   300
Kilometres

"Endurance"
beset
18 Jan 1915

slept or huddled below, the other divided the tasks of steering at the tiller, handling the sail, and bailing water. When it was time for one group to go below deck and the second to take their turn on duty, Shackleton had to direct each man where to crawl so that they did not collide with one another. It was crucial that the switch went smoothly. The weather was subject to quick and unexpected changes, and high winds could give rise to destructive gales in mere moments. The men did not need to be told that the sea could be lethal, but they were re-minded nonetheless when they saw wreckage from an old ship floating past them.

Each day they scanned the skies anxiously for a glimpse of the sun. Without it, Worsley could not make the calculations necessary to navi-gate. He could determine their position by using a sextant, a triangular, hand-held instrument. By looking through the sextant at the sun and the horizon, he could determine the angle between the two. Once he had calculated this figure, he recorded the precise time of day using a chronometer, which is an extremely accurate timepiece. With these pieces of information, Worsley could then use his navigational charts to determine their precise position and to chart the course, or direction, that they needed to take. Accuracy was extremely important, and quite difficult for Worsley, trying to peer through the sextant at both horizon and sun while the boat climbed up and down the waves, all the while rolling from side to side. It was like trying to take a reading of the sun's position from a roller coaster.

To remain as steady as possible, Worsley would brace himself on

A map following the route of the *Endurance,* from Shackleton's book *South.*

The dotted line shows the course Worsley intended to follow to reach

South Georgia.

Captain Frank Worsley. Without his brilliant navigation, the crew of the *Caird* would probably have perished.

deck with both legs, while two men held him in place, one on each side. He would take the reading just as the *Caird* reached the top of a wave, allowing him a brief unobscured view of the horizon. It was a difficult process that had to be repeated often, sometimes many times in one day. It was the only way to know not only how far they had come but exactly in which direction they had to sail.

Toward the end of the first week, they began to grow used to the strange lurching of the boat. It remained relatively still when they were between waves, then madly rushed skyward as they hurtled to a wave's peak. Once on top, there was a brief pause when it seemed the entire ocean was at their feet. Seconds later they would plummet down the wave like an out-of-control skier, until they reached the calm water in the valley between crests. There they awaited the next wave, and the pattern repeated itself again and again, all day and night, until it seemed quite natural to them.

Shackleton made sure that each day was structured with routine. Every morning a pot of steaming hoosh was carefully prepared by Crean, who acted as cook. The shivering men eagerly awaited his cry of "Hoosh!" which signaled that the hot stew was ready. Food was eaten at near scalding temperatures to help keep up their body temperatures.

Though the conditions were more extreme than the crew could have imagined, they doggedly pressed on with deliberate cheerfulness.

Worsley was always amused by McCarthy, who greeted the captain each day by remarking, "It's a fine day, sir!" no matter how dark the skies and how vicious the winds. Crean spent each turn at the tiller singing enthusiastically, and there was much debate as to the identity of the tune he sang over and over. The saying "grin and bear it" became their motto, the guiding principle by which they lived.

In the sub-Antarctic ocean, stormy gales are frequent. The *Caird* sailed into a serious one toward the end of their first week at sea. Temperatures dropped substantially, so the waves breaking over the *Caird* froze, causing the boat to become completely encased in ice. Even the sails froze, and with the extra weight of the ice, the *Caird* was in danger of sinking. The ice had to be removed as quickly as it appeared. The gale lasted three days, and for each of these days the men took turns working frantically to chip the ice off the boat with any tools avail-

Tom Crean, one of the five men who accompanied Shackleton on the boat journey to South Georgia.

able. It was a dangerous business, for the ice made all sections of the boat lethally slick, and there would be no hope of retrieving a man who had fallen overboard in those stormy conditions. The waves were so high that they gave the impression the *Caird* was surrounded by a towering wall of water. Hanging on to the boat while chopping at the ice with his free hand, Worsley looked like a rodeo cowboy atop a bucking bronco. He spent so much time crouched on deck that he froze into that position, his tired muscles locked in place. His companions had to open him up, as he put it, like a jackknife, and rub his arms and legs back to life.

There was little hope of rest, even for those off duty below. It was impossible to get any comfort inside the soaked sleeping bags. Several of the bags were beginning to smell so awful they had to be tossed overboard. There was nothing to do but huddle miserably and wait for the storm to subside. On May 2, three days after it began, the gale fell off, and a warm sun peeked through. To the men, it was a small miracle. May 3 brought sunny skies and warm temperatures, and the men felt really good for the first time since leaving Elephant Island. Worsley took advantage of the weather to take a reading on their position. His findings thoroughly thrilled them all. With the help of the gale, they had come 444 miles. It was their tenth day aboard, and they had passed the halfway mark. The sun on their faces, their soaked possessions spread over the boat to dry, and half of the trip behind them, they began really to believe that they were going to succeed. With hard work and a little luck, the captain felt they should reach South Georgia in less than a week.

The seasonable weather could not last long, and on May 5 another gale blew up, causing the wind to create two sets of waves that crossed from opposite directions. The resulting motion of the ship caused even more discomfort, both above and below deck, than usual. Taking his turn at the tiller that evening, Shackleton looked up and was pleased to see a patch of light, clear sky overhead. As he was calling below to tell the men of the clearing weather, he glanced up again and was struck dumb in midsentence. What he had taken for clear skies was in fact the white-crested top of a wave so huge it blotted out all view of the horizon and sky. Shackleton later remarked that in twenty-six years of sea travel, he had never encountered such a gigantic wave.

This was a rogue wave—an unexplained surge of water reaching almost unbelievable heights. Sir Ernest barely had time to shout a frantic warning to the men before the wave slammed furiously onto the *Caird*.

The boat seemed to be rising and sinking at the same time, speeding through a solid wall of green sea and white foam. The *Caird* was swamped with water, and they bailed with whatever they could grab, some simply cupping their hands and splashing the water out. Just one more wave of that size would finish them off, but none came. The huge sea mountain thundered past them like a freight train and continued its rampage into the night. The *Caird* sailed on.

CHAPTER THIRTEEN

A Life Left Behind

Aт some point Shackleton's thoughts must have turned to all he had given up for this voyage—and all he had left behind. The parting that caused him the most pain, and on which he most often dwelled, was with his wife, Emily. They were introduced to each other in 1897, but it was seven long years before they married. During that time, Shackleton fought to win her affection, and later her father's approval, with as much passion and determination as he had ever put forth in the Antarctic. It was clear that he was completely devoted to her, and she never swayed in her unquestioning loyalty to and support of her famous husband. He was never more keenly aware of his feelings for her than when departing on one of his trips.

During his British Antarctic expedition of 1907, as he began the first leg of his journey south, he wrote to Emily (whom he nicknamed Child), "My Darling Wife, your dear brave face is before me now and I can see you just as you stand on the wharf and are smiling at me—my heart was too full to speak and I felt that I wanted just to come ashore and clasp you in my arms and love and care for you: Child, honestly and truly it was the worst heart aching moment in my life."

She always waited for him, and though when away he often was quick to develop affections for other women, he always came back to her. Their time at home together, however, was not always happy. Though Shackleton longed for the warmth of his home and his wife's company when he was on an expedition, when actually there he sometimes felt confined and restless. The Shackletons had three children, Raymond, Cecily, and the youngest, Edward. Their father plainly adored them, but he had great plans for their futures and, as a result, could be an unintentionally domineering and harsh parent. And then there was the question of money.

Shackleton was never without a plan to gain immediate and certain wealth, but so far, none of those plans had actually produced any riches. On his 1909 return from his British Antarctic expedition, he had become an instant celebrity, recognized and cheered wherever he traveled as the man who had come closer than any other to the South Pole. He became a favorite of King Edward VII, who knighted him that same year in honor of his polar achievements. He had been wined and dined all over the country. None of this, however, brought him any income. The Shackletons and their three children were surviving solely on a modest annual income that Emily had been left by her father. Shackleton felt very deeply his failure to provide financial support to his family.

It was not for lack of trying. Somehow, though, Shackleton had an uncanny knack for failing in his business ventures. In the years leading up to the *Endurance* expedition, he had tried his hand at journalism and industry, dabbled in politics, and had become involved with ventures ranging from boat chartering to gold mines. Ernest and Emily had initially established a household in Scotland, following Shackleton's securing a job as the secretary of the Scottish Royal Geographical Society. Neither the job nor their home was to be permanent. Although they did not change homes as often as Shackleton changed professions, they moved to various towns within reach of London. Each time he was certain that treasure was within his grasp. Never once did he succeed in touching it. He was only able to get his feet firmly under him, it seemed, on the Antarctic ice. Unfortunately, that too cost money.

In addition to his wife and children, Shackleton had left behind a number of people to whom he owed money for his expedition costs. The year before setting sail in the *Endurance,* he had run constantly from one man to another, seeking to borrow or be given the money he needed to equip and carry out his expedition. It was said during that time that one of the most important qualities of a polar explorer was that he be a good beggar. Shackleton, with his tremendously forceful and attractive personality, was an excellent one. Enormously entertaining, modest, fascinating, and warm-hearted, he was incapable of false flattery or contrived behavior. All kinds of people, from servants to wealthy business magnates, found him irresistible. He was as well liked an explorer as the world had ever known. His considerable efforts to raise funds, though personally exhausting, were always successful in the end. As with his 1907 expedition, a last-minute donation from a wealthy individual gave him the money he needed to set sail in the *Endurance,* but the bills were piling up. They would all have to be dealt with at the expedition's close.

Emily bore these difficulties admirably. Time and time again she allowed her husband to leave her and the children, saying only, "One must not chain down an eagle in a barnyard." She was truly a remarkable woman and worthy of Shackleton's deep love. As he often told her, it was his life's ambition to make himself worthy of her.

These were the circumstances he had left behind him, and at times they pressed so heavily on Shackleton's conscience that they seemed capable of dragging him to the icy ocean floor. Because of them, and in spite of them, Shackleton defiantly struggled to stay afloat.

CHAPTER FOURTEEN

South Georgia

THE FOLLOWING MORNING PUT THE *CAIRD* JUST ONE hundred miles from South Georgia. The men could not arrive soon enough. Their hands were blackened and scarred by blisters, frostbite, and burns from the little stove. Their legs were numb and swollen from the icy water. One of their kegs of water had spoiled after a hole in the container had let in some seawater. This contaminated supply was their only remaining drinking water, and they had to filter each sip through gauze to remove as much salt as possible. Drinking salt water could cause serious illness, and each man was already too weak to withstand more physical hardship. Still, with each hour they sensed they were growing closer to their goal.

By the fourteenth day, they knew the island might soon be visible, but a thick mist made it difficult for Worsley to get a reading from the sun. Navigational accuracy was as important now as it had been on the trip to Elephant Island, and for similar reasons. Even a small error could cause them to miss the island, and the prevailing westerlies and currents would prevent them from backtracking. If they were off by a larger margin, they might sail past South Georgia without ever seeing it. It might be days or weeks before they realized their error, and except for a

South Georgia's
forbidding coast.

few tiny islands in the middle of the Atlantic Ocean, there was no further landfall until Africa.

When the sun rose the following morning, Shackleton was pleased to see seaweed floating in the water and birds circling overhead. Both of these signs were good indications that land was not far away. Sure enough, later that day a jubilant McCarthy caught sight of a cliff rising out of the sea in the distance. Two weeks after the men set sail, South Georgia was at last within view. Speechless with delight, the men simply sat and grinned at each other. They were going to make it.

By sunset they were just eighteen miles away, but with the coming darkness they had to heave to, using the wind and sails to halt the boat in the water, until morning. They fully expected to make landfall the following day, but perhaps their experience should have told them the worst was yet to come. In a maddening repeat of the events they experienced after sighting Elephant Island, a hurricane blew up and threatened to crush the boat before she could land. Like all experienced sailors, they knew they were in as much danger of sinking while trying to land as they had been in the open ocean. From their position, South Georgia lay behind a reef of sharp and treacherous rocks that lined the coast like teeth. The *Caird* inched along the coast, looking for a gap in the rocks big enough to pass through.

It was as if the sea had sensed they were beating it and grew vengeful. The hurricane was driving them inland, straight for the jagged reef. If they were swept onto the rocks, they would sink instantly. There was little they could do but hang on and try to keep a small measure of control over the boat. The wind howled and nudged them closer and closer to the reef, while the waves broke over them. Worsley described the conditions as the most dangerous he had ever sailed in. Even Shackleton, the eternal optimist, prepared to die. As evening grew closer, Worsley felt not so much fear as anger that no one would ever know how far they had come and that his own painstakingly maintained diary would now be lost along with their lives.

By nightfall, without warning, the hurricane slipped away as quickly as it had come. Almost afraid to believe it, the men waited out the night. The next morning, with little fanfare, they crept ashore, and within minutes they were standing on land. South Georgia's glaciers meant fresh water to drink, and its whaling stations meant life.

They found a little cave nearby, and the men drank hot milk while stretched out inside their sleeping bags. As the others dropped off to sleep, Shackleton sat alone outside, keeping watch over their boat.

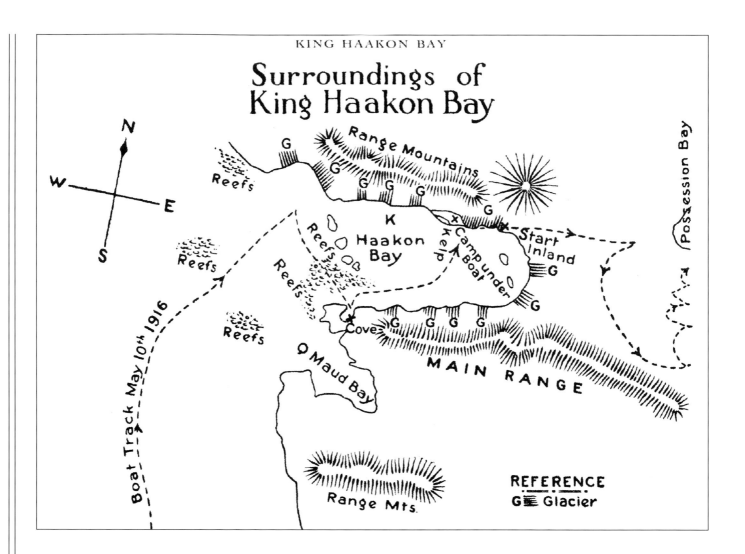

Surroundings of King Haakon Bay

A map from the original edition of Shackleton's *South,* showing the *Caird's* approach to South Georgia.

Before him the sea rose and fell. At his back lay the massive glaciers and ice-covered mountains of South Georgia. The Stromness whaling station, their best hope for rescue, lay clear on the other side of the island. Though he had brought his men safely to land, Sir Ernest knew that they were far from completing their journey. Yesterday's experience had proved that they could not hope to sail safely around the island to the Stromness whaling station. McNeish, McCarthy, and Vincent were all extremely weak and could not travel far. Shackleton's only option was to reach the station on foot. This meant walking from one end of the island to the other, crossing the glaciers and mountain range in between. No one had ever attempted to do this before and with good reason. It was common knowledge to the whalers and seamen living on the island, and to Shackleton himself, that the mountains could not be climbed.

Staring out at the ocean, Shackleton knew he had no choice but to try to prove them wrong.

CHAPTER FIFTEEN

Across Uncharted Mountains

Shackleton and his small crew rested on the shore of King Haakon Bay for several days. If he could have immediately gone on, Shackleton undoubtedly would have done so. He knew, however, that even he needed to rest and recover for several days before he would be strong enough to begin the trek over the mountains to the Stromness whaling station. Sometime later, Shackleton confided to Worsley that he had felt one more day in the boat would have killed them, so weak was their condition.

Their cave was small but well suited to their needs. They arranged their sleeping bags in a tight circle around the fire and spent the next few days leisurely, leaving the cave only to hunt for food or to investigate their surroundings. A stream provided fresh drinking water, and a local colony of albatross, a large seafaring bird, provided a supply of food. All they lacked was blubber to fuel their fire and stove. After months on the ice, camping on the harsh beach on Elephant Island, and two weeks of wet and frozen conditions on the *Caird*, the cave was like a palace. The *Caird*'s sails were draped over the entrance like curtains, keeping everything inside warm and dry. It was impossible to relax completely, however, knowing their companions back on Elephant Island were enjoying no such luxurious conditions.

The cave was located beneath an enormous range of cliffs that blocked any possible starting route for the journey overland. They would have to sail a short distance across the bay to find a better starting place, but not before regaining some of their strength. Their minds needed to rest just as badly as their bodies. The second night in the cave, Worsley was awakened by Shackleton's booming voice shouting warnings, his finger pointing off into the darkness. Worsley realized that Shackleton was dreaming that he was still aboard the *Caird*, watching the monster wave crash down on them again.

Feeling stronger each day, Shackleton and Worsley made more trips outside the cave to examine the landscape and hunt for food. They found a large pile of driftwood and wreckage from ships that had been sunk trying to round Cape Horn, a thousand miles away. The remains of these ships had been caught in a peculiar current and swept onshore at this spot, a dark reminder of those who had not been as lucky as they. On a happier note, they found and killed an elephant seal; its blubber would provide fuel for their stove. Since they had not brought a gun on their walk, Worsley had to kill the seal with a large stone, and he ripped his shirt and covered himself with blood in the process. Shackleton had not lost his famous sense of humor and insisted on playing a joke on their companions. Staggering back to the cave, he told the men that Worsley had hurled himself at a seal that was charging Shackleton and that he had saved Shackleton's life. No one believed the imaginative story, but they were well pleased to see the meat and blubber.

They were now strong enough to make the short journey across the bay in the *Caird*. King Haakon Bay was a U-shaped inlet of ocean, surrounded on three sides by land. It was therefore fairly sheltered from

South Georgia's seals served as food and fuel for Shackleton and his five exhausted men.

the stormy seas surrounding the island. Since Shackleton only needed to sail from one side of the bay to the other, he would avoid the dangerous waves and reef that had almost prevented them from landing on the island. From their new position they would be a few miles closer to the whaling station and in a place where Shackleton could more easily begin his walk across the island. The men were not happy to leave their cozy little cave, but they knew it would be a short and uneventful journey to their new camp. The boat trip was almost not made at all, because the *Caird*'s rudder, or steering device, had been knocked off the boat during their landing and had floated away. Much to Shackleton's surprise, the rudder washed up onshore later, almost exactly where he was standing. Shackleton marveled that in the whole of the vast ocean, the rudder had chosen to reappear at his feet. Without it, they could not have steered the *Caird* and would have been unable to make the brief boat journey. It was another strange and lucky event that could not be explained.

They crossed the bay in the *Caird*, singing most of the way, with no complications. As there was no cave to be found at their new position, they made a camp beneath the overturned *Caird* similar to the shelter on Elephant Island. Shackleton and Worsley took a few walks over the area and made a rough plan of direction for the hike to Stromness. Because no one had ever crossed the mountains, the way across South Georgia was completely unmapped. They had no idea what lay ahead of them, or what might stand in their way.

McNeish and Vincent were greatly weakened, and McCarthy was not doing much better. It was decided that these three would stay behind in the shelter, while Shackleton, Worsley, and Crean made the hike to Stromness. Once to the station, Shackleton would be able to send a sturdy and seaworthy whaling vessel back to pick them up.

Conditions on the march to Stromness would be difficult enough without the added complications of wind and snow. What they did know about the island was that a range of mountains, some of them up to six thousand feet high, crossed it from one side to the other. The rocky peaks would be favorite targets of the gale force winds, which could pluck a man off a mountain face in a heartbeat. Keeping this in mind, they waited over a week for the perfect weather for their departure.

On May 18, the weather had cleared completely. They set off well before dawn of the next day, the snowy landscape fully lit by the moon. They carried with them enough supplies to last each man for three days. If their luck and the weather held, they should make it to Stromness in half that time. Included in their supplies were a small portable cooker, binoculars, a compass, matches, rope, and a small axe. It was important to travel light. Because no one had ever crossed the mountains, and no maps existed, they would have to proceed by trial and error. This meant climbing mountain after mountain until they found a way down and across to the other side.

After a handshake and a few parting words with each man, Shackleton, Worsley, and Crean left their companions and began walking up the first steep ascent. Ahead in the moonlight, Shackleton could see a dark area where the snow had broken away, leaving a crevasse in the snow. Crevasses, or deep pockets in the snow or ice, were often covered by a thin layer of snow that gave the illusion of solid ground. Shackleton had encountered his share of these crevasses in his expeditions in Antarctica, and he knew how dangerous they were. Once a man fell into one, there was very little chance of getting him out again. They roped themselves together for safety and proceeded in single file. In this way, if the first man fell into a crevasse, the two men behind him could dig in their heels and break his fall, pulling him back out with the rope. It was still a dangerous business, and hoping to avoid crevasses altogether, they moved with great caution.

By dawn, they found a way down to a large frozen lake about three thousand feet below them. Making their way carefully down the slope and over a stretch of glacier, they reached the lake some time later, only to find it was not a lake at all. Instead, it was the sea. They had gone too far east and had to retrace their steps for two hours back up the three-thousand-foot peak. On several occasions, they had to turn around and go back down a steep slope they had just climbed, because there was no

way down the other side. These were the kinds of mistakes they could not afford to make. Time was too precious to waste.

By nine in the morning, they had been on the move for six hours. They stopped for a meal of hot hoosh and stared at the mountain peaks in the distance while they ate. This was the mountain range they had to cross in order to reach Stromness. Between the peaks was a series of four gaps, or passes. They would need to find a way through one of

A glacier on South Georgia. Shackleton, Worsley, and Crean crossed several such glaciers.

these gaps, and a walkable path down the other side. Once past this mountain range, they hoped the most difficult part of the walk would be behind them.

Feeling strengthened by the hot meal, they walked to the base of the mountain and climbed up in the direction of the first pass. When they reached the pass, they saw at once that they could not get over it—there was a straight drop down the other side. Climbing part of the way back down, they inched their way sideways, then back up to the next pass. There they found the same sheer drop preventing them from going farther. There was no choice but to climb down and come up again to the third pass. This one, too, proved a dead end with no possible route down the other side. As they made their way toward the fourth pass, they realized the situation was becoming serious. They had now spent hours climbing and reclimbing the mountain in search of a way through to the other side. The sun was beginning to set, and the temperature was dropping quickly. It was one thing to travel through the lower land by moonlight, but Shackleton knew they could never live through the night at such a great height on the mountain, at the mercy of bitter cold and wind. They had spent too much time searching for a passable route, and one way or the other, they had to get off the mountain quickly.

Reaching the fourth gap, they found with dismay a similar steep drop down the other side, but far below they could see a flat snow surface. The sun had now set, and there was no time to retrace their steps back down the way they had come. The way down in front of them was far too steep to descend completely by foot. However, they could not stay put, or they would freeze to death in a matter of hours. Shackleton knew they were in a hopeless situation, so he must have felt there was simply nothing more to lose when he ordered his men to sit on the snow, one behind the other, and slide down the mountain face toboggan style.

At first, they thought he had lost his sense of reason. More likely than not it would be suicide to slide down the slope. There was no way to know in the growing darkness if the way was clear, or if they would fly off a cliff into the air or collide full force with a wall of stone. Crean and Worsley soon accepted the strange logic, however, that it was better to slide when it might kill them, than to stay put when doing so would undoubtedly kill them.

One seated behind the next, arms and legs wrapped around the waist of the man in front, they took off down the mountain like a shot. They were flying blind. They hurtled downward at a frightening rate, shouting and screeching like boys on a roller coaster. It had been an agonizing and exhilarating two minutes when they sensed the slope beneath them was becoming less steep. With a thud, they plopped into a soft snow bank. For a moment they sat, quite stunned, not realizing it was over. Then silence gave way to celebration, and they laughed hysterically to find themselves safe after their heart-stopping ride. Worsley later estimated they had dropped an entire mile.

With little time to waste congratulating each other, they had a quick meal, then edged up another slope in front of them. The moon began to rise, throwing a path of clear light before them. As they were constantly moving, the cold seemed quite bearable. At midnight, twenty-one hours after leaving camp, they reached the top and paused to eat before picking their way down.

Shackleton allowed for one hot meal every four hours. Other than eating and the occasional brief rest, they were walking virtually around the clock. Still, they were in good spirits, and Worsley and Crean sang cheerfully as the small fire burned within the stove, heating their precious hoosh to the boiling point.

Later, both Crean and Worsley fell asleep during one of the short breaks. Shackleton forced himself to stay awake. He knew, as did all explorers of icy climates, that to fall asleep in freezing conditions was a

dangerous thing. The sleeper, experiencing the increasing cold, interprets the numbness as warmth, and continues to sleep until freezing to death. Shackleton waited ten minutes, then woke them, telling them they had slept for one half hour. The white lie worked—both Crean and Worsley felt greatly rested.

By 6 A.M. on May 20, they reached the gap at the top of the last steep slope and began making their way down past the last of the mountains. Before the *Endurance* left for Antarctica they had visited Stromness, and by now they were beginning to recognize some of the countryside in the distance. They were heading in the right direction, and the worst of the

A panoramic photograph of South Georgia and its mountain range.

terrain lay behind them. Worsley guessed they had only twelve miles left to walk.

At 7 A.M., they heard a noise that froze them in their tracks. In the distance, the unmistakable shriek of the Stromness steam whistle was sounding the morning wake-up call. This noise, which to their ears was divine music, confirmed that they were on the brink of civilization. It was a moment both serious and delightful. There was no doubt now. They were going to make it.

Though there were no more mountains to be climbed, it wasn't exactly easy going. On the descent to Stromness they encountered a slope of solid ice so steep it seemed to go almost straight down. They made their way down it lying flat on their backs, cutting steps into the ice with their axe and with the heels of their boots. Following this descent they crossed a relatively flat surface, discovering it to be a lake only when the ice gave way and Crean dropped into the water.

By 1:30 in the afternoon they reached the final ridge of high land. Climbing to the top, they could see the buildings and grounds of Stromness below. They marched down a natural path made by the V-shape of two adjoining hills. It was wet going, as the melted snow and ice from each slope flowed downhill underfoot. The water was sometimes as high as their knees, and their legs became numb and clumsy. What lay before them was more discouraging. The path suddenly steepened, then disappeared. Here, less than a mile from the whaling station, nature had seen fit to form a waterfall.

It looked to be about a thirty-foot drop, hemmed in on either side by the steep slopes. It simply wasn't possible to turn back now. Shackleton didn't give anyone much time to think. He tied a rope around a rock, and they plunged in. One at a time, they lowered themselves down the rope through a torrent of frigid water.

At the bottom, they stood on flat, solid ground. Not even the icy dunking could dim their soaring spirits. They were just minutes away from Stromness. Shackleton was surprised to see Worsley hesitating. On closer investigation, he found his captain was taking the opportunity to fuss over his own appearance. There wasn't much that could be done to remove the months of accumulated grime and filth, so Worsley contented himself with piecing his ragged clothes together with three safety pins he had saved. Shackleton was much amused by this sad effort and teased him about it for years to come.

Moments later, they walked onto the station grounds. It was now afternoon, and most of the men were working. The first few who caught sight of the three men hurried away without speaking. The travelers were hardly surprised. They had become accustomed to each other's appearances but knew that their long tangled hair and beards, filthy faces and clothes, must make for an unpleasant appearance—and an even worse smell. Shackleton tried to ask two boys for directions to the manager's quarters, but the boys took one look and scampered off like a pair of frightened deer. Finally, Shackleton stopped one of the Norwegian sailors, who directed them to the home of the station manager, Thoralf Sørlle. Shackleton and Sørlle had been friends, but on opening his door, Sørlle stared at Sir Ernest without recognition.

There are different stories about what happened next. Worsley remembered Sørlle denying he knew them, until Shackleton revealed his name. Shackleton recalled Sørlle confusing him with another man. A sailor standing next to Sørlle said that upon hearing Shackleton give his name, Sørlle began to weep with amazement and shock. Whatever happened, all agree that Sørlle quickly took the three men into his home. He gave them food and drink. The three men had never tasted such sweetness. While they feasted, Sørlle sat, his eyes huge, as Shackleton told his story.

CHAPTER SIXTEEN

A Plan for Rescue

As the men took turns bathing, Sørlle quickly made arrangements for a whaling boat to be sent around the coast for the three men at King Haakon Bay. A freshly bathed and cleanly clothed Worsley accompanied the whaler on the trip. He happily said that every misery they had endured seemed worthwhile after the incredible pleasure the hot bath had brought to his aching bones. The whaler departed that evening and by the following morning had arrived at King Haakon Bay.

In the makeshift camp, McCarthy heard the sound of the rescue boat's whistle. He waved and shouted as a small rowboat was launched to pick them up. The three men, though thrilled to be found, expressed disappointment that Captain Worsley had not come for them himself. This caused Worsley, who was standing right in front of them, to burst into laughter. Scrubbed clean, with new clothes, a shave, and a haircut, Worsley was unrecognizable to his companions of the last sixteen months.

Back at Stromness, Shackleton spent his first night in civilization in

such comfort he found himself unable to fall asleep. Through the window, he watched as snow began to fall heavily. If they had encountered such snowy conditions the night before on their trek, they could not

The reportedly impassable mountains of South Georgia.

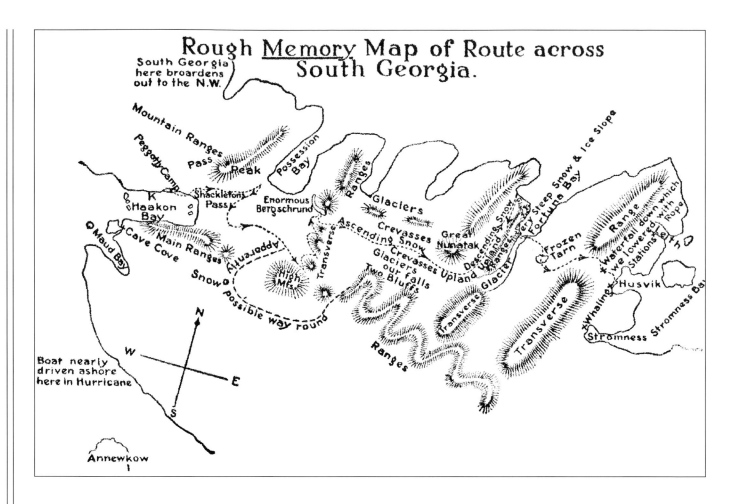

Rough Memory Map of Route across South Georgia.

A map from the original edition of Shackleton's *South,* showing the route over South Georgia.

have made it over the mountains. Long into the night, Shackleton lay in the soft warmth, watching the storm and feeling thankful.

More than thirty years later, a professional mountaineer made the same journey over South Georgia's mountains, equipped with an experienced crew and all of the food, clothing, and climbing gear they required. His was the second expedition ever to cross the mountains. Of Shackleton's group, the man said, "I do not know how they did it, except that they had to."

The following evening, with the six men from the *Caird* now reunited, a great gathering was held. A large number of old sailors, mostly

Norwegian, had come to shake hands with the men who had accomplished the impossible. Most of them had spent their adult lives sailing these stormy southern seas, and none of them had ever heard of such an astonishing journey as the *Caird* had made.

Though it was near heaven to be in the company of other people again, Shackleton was extremely anxious to return to Elephant Island to rescue the rest of his men. Privately, he feared that some of the weaker ones might have already died.

A large whaling vessel called the *Southern Sky* was spending the winter in the Stromness harbor. Shackleton quickly got permission to borrow the ship for the rescue journey to Elephant Island. There was no shortage of crew; in the tradition of sea rescue, the whaling men eagerly volunteered to come along and help.

The *Southern Sky* was quickly prepared and, under steam power, made its way in the direction of Elephant Island. On their approach, they found no way through the pack ice, which had grown thicker with the coming of winter. Running low on fuel, a devastated Shackleton turned around only sixty miles from the island. He took the *Southern Sky* to the Falkland Islands, off the coast of South America, and immediately planned a second rescue attempt. It was now late May—one and a half months since leaving Elephant Island in the *Caird*. Time was slipping away.

From the Falklands, Shackleton was able to send telegrams communicating their situation to the outside world. Word was immediately gotten to his wife and, as soon as he could, he wrote to Emily himself. He briefly told her what had happened, assured her of his safety, and added, "It was nature against us the whole time." She received the news of his safety with great relief. Months turned into years of waiting for word of his safe return had made Lady Shackleton as strong willed and durable as the Antarctic had made her husband. Though he vowed

Stromness whaling
station.

otherwise, she knew in her heart that he could not intend to end his exploration career now. If there was a way on earth for her husband to return again to Antarctica, he would find the way to do so. At home, running the household and raising their children almost single-handedly, Lady Shackleton quietly went on with her life. In all the disappointment Shackleton was to encounter in his life, he could at least feel sheer satisfaction in the capabilities and strength of the woman he had married.

The world celebrated the news of Shackleton's safety. Even in the midst of the war, which was still raging, he made headlines. He received a cable from the king of England, congratulating him and expressing all hopes that his men would soon be safe. All the while, Shackleton was involved in a frantic attempt to locate another boat for the second rescue attempt. He soon located the *Instituto de Pesca No. 1*. After some hasty preparations it set out for Elephant Island with Shackleton aboard. It took just three days, and the peaks of Elephant Island were in sight, but again the iron blanket of pack ice would not let them through. Almost sick with frustration, Shackleton had no choice but to turn back.

Shackleton traveled on board a mail boat to the nearby country of Chile. With the help of a British government official, money was quickly raised to charter an oak schooner called the *Emma*. Equipped with sails and an engine that ran on oil, the *Emma* seemed to have the power and strength needed to penetrate the ice. This soon proved to be untrue. Within one hundred miles of Elephant Island, the *Emma,* too, was turned back by the ice. It had now been close to three months since Shackleton had reached Stromness, and yet he seemed no closer to rescuing his men. Shackleton was growing frantic, afraid that his men on the island would run out of food and starve to death before he could reach them. In truth, though he could not know it, this was very close to happening.

Returning to Chile, Shackleton received word that his old ship *Discovery* would arrive in six weeks and was his to use for the next attempt. Feeling strongly that his men could not survive that long, he pleaded with the government officials to lend him another boat. Finally, he was given the use of a small boat made of steel called the *Yelcho*. It was not a good choice for icy conditions, but Shackleton seized the opportunity, and on August 25 the fourth rescue attempt sailed out to sea.

At last Shackleton found what he sought—a gap in the pack ice. The *Yelcho* passed through, and in spite of the thick fog, they located

Elephant Island in the distance. As they sailed closer, Shackleton stood on deck scanning the coast for sight of his men. Worsley stood at his side. With his keen navigator's eyes, Worsley spotted the men's camp, and the *Yelcho* made straight for it as Shackleton squinted anxiously through his binoculars, looking for signs of life.

CHAPTER SEVENTEEN

"Are You All Well?"

THE MEN HAD GROWN THIN BENEATH THEIR SHELTER on the shores of Elephant Island. Each day Wild urged them to prepare their belongings for rescue, with the familiar cry of "Lash up and stow, boys, the Boss may come today!" Four months after Shackleton sailed off in search of help, even Wild no longer believed he was coming back for them.

Their spirits falling, hopes of rescue all but gone, and Shackleton as good as dead, the men glumly followed the same routine day after day. On August 30, all were present in the shelter for lunch except for Hurley and the expedition artist, Marston, who had wandered off on a short walk. Staring out at the ocean, which was covered in a gray mist, they were astonished to see what appeared to be a boat loom into view. Stunned, Marston began to shout, but no one emerged from the shelter. The men heard him, but given the hour, they assumed he was calling for lunch, and they ignored him.

Frantically, Marston ran down the path and skidded through the door of the shelter. The men continued to eat, until Marston, finding his shaking voice, cried out that he had seen a ship. Utter craziness followed. They all tried to get out the door at the same time and ripped

Performing daily chores on Elephant Island helped distract the men, who by now had grown desperate for rescue.

down the canvas walls in their haste to get outside. Someone carried Blackborrow, who still couldn't walk after his frostbite operation. Several men were so excited they ran into the snow in their bare feet, not even noticing the cold.

Wild carried a pile of clothing and some fuel to the top of the hill, where he quickly made a signal fire. He needn't have bothered. On the deck of the *Yelcho*, Shackleton and Worsley had already seen them. A

rowboat was lowered over the side of the *Yelcho,* and once on the sea, Shackleton climbed into it. Even from a great distance, his powerful shape was unmistakable. The men onshore recognized him instantly, and the group erupted with screams and cheers.

Shackleton himself was not yet celebrating. As the boat pulled closer to the shore, he tensely counted the men, then recounted. When he was within earshot, he leaned over the side of the rowboat and called

Shortly after the sighting of the rescue ship, *Yelcho.* A signal fire is still burning at left.

strongly, "Are you all well?" Wild's voice quickly boomed back, assuring him that every one of them was alive and safe. The fear that had been torturing Shackleton for months was laid to rest. He had not lost a single life.

The excited and bedraggled men swarmed around Shackleton as the

boat landed. They wanted to show him their shelter, their lookout point, and everything they had made. But Shackleton, desperately afraid the pack ice would close in on them once again, refused. Dividing the party into two groups, he rushed each man into the rowboat, and they turned and began to pull quickly for the *Yelcho*, hovering dimly in the distance.

In Shackleton's book *South*, this photo is captioned "All Safe! All Well!" Shackleton himself is in the rowboat pulling for shore.

· · ·

On September 3, 1916, almost two years after the *Endurance* first raised
her sails and pushed toward Antarctica, Sir Ernest Shackleton fulfilled a
vow he had made to himself many months before. He brought every
one of the *Endurance* men, alive and well, out of Antarctica and back to
the world that waited to welcome them as heroes.

EPILOGUE

IN THE GREAT HISTORY OF ANTARCTICA, SIR ERNEST Shackleton is not the most famous explorer. His onetime leader, Robert Scott, and Roald Amundsen are the continent's most recognized and revered children. Amundsen and Scott both reached the South Pole, something that Shackleton in his lifetime never accomplished. But it is Shackleton's story that is the most spectacular. In many ways his accomplishments outshine the others, for they were won in the face of failure, and in spite of it. What happened to him, and what he did about it, is simply unbelievable, and yet it is all true. He had the very best and the very worst luck of any man alive. And yet there were times when it seemed that something more than luck had a hand in the survival of Shackleton and his men.

In addition to the strange quirks of fate, the premonitions of danger, the path appearing in the ice, and other such occurrences, there was something else that Shackleton didn't talk about right away. During the journey over South Georgia, Sir Ernest was constantly under the impression that there was a fourth man with them, yet no such man existed. In a discussion with Worsley, and a later discussion with Crean, Shackleton learned that each of them had also felt the presence of a fourth man. If Shackleton thought he knew who the fourth man might be, he never said so. It remains a mysterious element in the plot of a most remarkable story.

Shackleton's immeasurable talent as a leader of men is unquestionable, but his greatness was tied to Antarctica and the giant steps he took there. Back in the "real" world, his footsteps seemed much smaller, and they led to debt, failed business ventures, and disappointment. Life in England could not deliver him what he desired. It was only in the other world of Antarctica that he seemed truly to become himself. It was as if the continent was his second half, and joined with it, he achieved greatness.

The world war would continue for another two years before finally coming to an exhausted conclusion in 1918. Shackleton immediately involved himself in the war, traveling to South America, and later Russia, to undertake war-related projects for his government. Even in the midst of these projects, however, he was not quite satisfied. The war came to a close, and still Shackleton longed to return to the southern continent once again.

In 1921, Shackleton found a benefactor willing to pay for another expedition to Antarctica. His plan was to sail his new ship, the *Quest,* around the entire continent. His old friends Worsley and Wild joined him on the voyage. Shackleton never reached Antarctica. On January 5, 1922, as the *Quest* idled in the harbor at South Georgia, Shackleton suffered a heart attack and died shortly thereafter. He was forty-seven years old.

At his wife's direction, Shackleton was buried there on South Georgia, where he had struggled and thrived so fully six years before. It seemed fitting that he remain there in the southern latitudes, where he had made his mark and been happiest. Of Shackleton's life, his friend and biographer Hugh Robert Mill wrote that "he lived like a mighty, rushing wind."

For all purposes, the Imperial Trans-Antarctic Expedition was a failure. Shackleton did not cross the continent of Antarctica. It would be another fifty years before someone was able to do it. Sir Edmund Hillary, the first man to climb Mount Everest, was on the expedition that finally accomplished the crossing. Of his predecessors, Hillary said, "For scientific discovery give me Scott; for speed and efficiency of travel give me Amundsen; but when disaster strikes and all hope is gone, get down on your knees and pray for Shackleton."

Had he known that the world would remember him this way, Sir Ernest Shackleton would most certainly have been pleased.

BIBLIOGRAPHY

Antarctica: Great Stories from the Frozen Continent. Surry Hills, New South Wales: Reader's Digest Books, 1985.

Fisher, Margery and Jay. *Shackleton and the Antarctic.* Cambridge, Mass.: James Barrie Books, 1957.

Huntford, Roland. *Shackleton.* New York: Hodder & Stoughton, 1985.

Imbert, Bertrand. *North Pole, South Pole: Journeys to the Ends of the Earth.* New York: Harry N. Abrams, Inc., 1992.

King, Peter, ed. *South,* by Sir Ernest Shackleton. London: Century, 1991.

Lansing, Alfred. Endurance: *Shackleton's Incredible Journey.* New York: Carroll & Graf Publishers, 1959.

Mill, Hugh Robert. *The Life of Sir Ernest Shackleton.* Boston: Little, Brown, and Company, 1923.

Shackleton, Sir Ernest. *South.* New York: Macmillan, 1920.

Worsley, Frank. *Shackleton's Boat Journey.* New York: W.W. Norton, 1977.

INDEX

Page numbers in *italics* refer to illustrations or captions.